Steam in Your Garden

Sir Edward Tapper out on the road. The shed staff have made a special effort to provide a spotless finish for the "pride of the line"

STEAM IN YOUR GARDEN

An Introduction to Live Steam Narrow
Gauge Railways for the Smaller Garden

by
Tag Gorton

The author's Longlands & Western Railway No 4 *Thomas Alfred* pauses at the tea rooms while proceeding light engine back to the shed on the South Hams Light Railway. Currently awaiting repair after an accident in transit, it is planned to receive a coat of Midland Red later in the year

ATLANTIC TRANSPORT PUBLISHERS
Trevithick House, West End, Penryn, Cornwall TR10 8HE

ISBN: O 906899 67 2

First published 1996

Unless otherwise credited, all photographs are by the author

Design and layout: Trevor Ridley

Printed in Great Britain

British Cataloguing in Publication Data
A catalogue record for this book is available from the British Library

Uniform with this volume: *Steam in Your Garden*

Contents

It's a slow, drowsy sort of summer afternoon as we sit drinking tea from our picnic thermos, close by a narrow gauge railway track in the West of England. The undulating rusty rails, just showing above the encroaching undergrowth, curve progressively away up the bank towards the hamlet of Trematon and a light breeze dapples the sunlight on the track beneath the trees. A gangers hut, disused these many years is subsiding gently back to nature and insects hum in the heather as a seagull watches us inquiringly from its perch on an outcrop of Cornish granite.

This rural idyll is broken by the unmistakable sound of a steam whistle which attracts our attention to a moving column of white steam charting the passage of a train through the distant cutting towards us, its busy chuffing giving a wholly unwarranted impression of speed. There is a low rumbling as the assemblage passes across the iron bridge over the River Lyner and a small, improbably Victorian locomotive hoves into view, all bustling side rods and tall chimney. The engine hunts and lurches over the rarely maintained track, piloting its train of assorted four and eight wheel coaches, all in various liveries and differing states of decrepitude.

The driver acknowledges our presence with a blip on the whistle, the exhaust sharpens as the regulator is opened for the assault on Trematon bank and the entourage of passenger stock grumbles past, jolting and swaying over the rail joints. A lone passenger peers disinterestedly at our little group from the faded and dusty red plush of a first class compartment as the string of vehicles follow the fussy green locomotive up the tree lined permanent way to Trematon. Steam drifts between the trees as the landscape reverts to its customary summer Sunday stillness and the evocative sound of the train dwindles into the distance.

An arcadian moment isn't it, taken not from a fading memory of Cornish yesteryear, but from a recent local meeting at the Longlands and Western Railway in my small back garden. The loco is my elderly and much modified radio controlled 16mm live steam Merlin Mayflower with steam whistle.

Real Steam Engines

For a very large number of garden rail enthusiasts the desire for live steam motive power has been the prime mover for constructing a model railway in the garden. Once upon a time this sort of project would have required considerable engineering skills, a capacious pocket and a lot of garden space. The construction of a standard gauge line in whatever scale commensurate with live steam would certainly be out of my financial range and, in any case, could not have been accommodated in my small back garden. It has only been in recent years that steam locomotives in a narrow gauge format have made it possible for railway modellers of moderate means and average ability to venture into the nowadays popular scenic scales of 16mm and G-scale.

The advantages of the narrow gauge format for a live steam railway are, in retrospect, immediately obvious. If we compare locomotives running on 0 gauge track it can be seen that a boiler of narrow gauge proportions to 16mm scale can be considerably larger than its 7mm counterpart. Cylinders will of course be larger and can be closer to scale while still providing a broad power band for comfortable running (when did you last see a live steam standard gauge locomotive in 7mm scale running at less than a scale 90 mph). If one is considering radio control then there is far more space on a narrow gauge loco to fit the requisite equipment. Narrow gauge, whatever the motive power, is of course eminently suitable for garden railways. Tight curves, modest stations and simple pointwork mean that all but the very smallest garden can accommodate one's own live steam railway.

It was some years ago that I first saw an example of a narrow gauge live steam model locomotive at a Plymouth model railway exhibition. Until seeing this 16mm scale narrow gauge steam engine chuffing round a temporary track under what appeared to be perfect radio control, I had always associated garden railways, and live steam in particular, with retired Admirals modelling main line practice in vast Surrey gardens. Nevertheless, here was an obviously controllable, narrow gauge real steam locomotive which could easily cope with tight curves. The idea of having a real steam train, on tap, in my small back garden became a possibility and my imagination was fired.

Now it may be that the more senior amongst us have memories of Bowman, Basset Lowke and various assorted pot boilers that would not function unless cigarette smoke was rising vertically from the Air Ministry roof! Others may be suspicious of the perceived engineering ethos of those who flirt with the miniature steam locomotive, and are wary of expensive

Steam drifts beneath the trees as *Sir George Harvey* spends a couple of hours shunting stock. This modified Merlin Meteor, with its close coupled drivers, is a stalwart of the line and happy with heavy trains

Activity at Longlands as station staff prepare for the afternoon "mixed" to Saltash Junction. These models stay out in the garden the year round

mistakes. I should like to set your mind at rest on both these points.

Radio Control

Modern radio controlled narrow gauge steam models, certainly those from major manufacturers such as Roundhouse or Pearse, are simple to use and reliable. Without doubt one does not have the track cleaning problems of two rail electric traction and my locomotives run happily in any weather that I will accept myself - and this has included snow, heavy rain or very windy conditions!

There is a leading manufacturer of fine 16mm and G scale locomotives, who badges his catalogue with the legend "Living Steam Railways" and this I can identify with. We all know of course that a steam locomotive, of whatever scale, is the "real thing". Nevertheless, I have never been attracted by the concentration of the model engineering societies on motive power to the exclusion of everything else. I am primarily a railway modeller who wishes to see steam trains running in a believable landscape, and the sight of a middle-aged man with his knees round his ears sitting behind a comparatively tiny locomotive I find faintly risible!

Longlands & Western

The sight and sound of my modified 16mm Merlin locomotive *Sir George Harvey* on the other hand, easing a heavy train through the reverse curves on the outskirts of Longlands station at a perfectly controlled scale ten miles an hour, with the steam drifting through the cutting and the sun dappling the ground cover beneath the miniature conifers I find is a perennial delight. With my Longlands and Western Railway and within a boundary of 30 x 20 feet, I try to portray the gently decaying ambience of a run down narrow gauge country backwater between the wars.

Most people who build steam powered railways in the garden, to what I call the "scenic" scales of 16mm and G are not model engineers at all, but are like myself, refugees from the table top railway. Comparatively few of us are capable of building a live steam locomotive but, like modellers in other scales we are on a permanent learning curve and certainly if one can put together an OO gauge building or rolling stock kit then the construction of a garden railway is not the major problem it might appear.

16mm Association

Perhaps the turning point of my vague steamy ambitions was when I joined the Association of 16mm Narrow Gauge Modellers which caters for both 16mm and G scale modellers. I am not naturally one of life's joiners but certainly this excellent fraternity provided me with a very professional magazine four times a year, the opportunity to meet local modellers (many of whom have become friends) and, importantly, hard information. I append the address below for those who are interested in membership.

One major advantage is of course the opportunity to see (and maybe try) steam engines in action at garden meetings all over the country - so much better than relying solely on advertisements or reviews! Certainly if you visit my small line in the West Country there would be an opportunity for you, and your offspring if they wish, to drive any of my locomotives. The youngest recorded driver on the Longlands and Western was a young lady of some four summers who actually made a better fist of it than her Dad!

Other sources of information include of course, *GardenRail*. This expanding magazine provides a very useful cross scale forum and while it largely deals with G and 16mm scale there is useful information to be gained from people's experience in other gauge/scale combinations right up to the "ride on" stuff! The G Scale Society of course specialises in their particular scale and offers similar opportunities to the 16mm Association. Perhaps however this Society leans toward electric motive power but has nevertheless, an interesting magazine and many members do run live steam locomotives. Again the address is below.

An American publication, *Steam in the Garden*, covers the steam motive power scene in the United States but has many regular contributors from this side of the pond and is available from Brandbright Ltd.

Many of you will be wondering just what is the difference between 16mm and G Scale. Both scale/gauge combinations are used for modelling narrow gauge prototypes. 16mm to the generally runs on track of 32mm gauge and is to a scale of 19.1 : 1 (16 mm to the foot). You will perhaps be aware that G scale trains run on rails that are 45 mm apart and I'm sure that you will have heard of LGB (Lehmann Gross Bahn) with its elephant proof track which uses a scale of 22.5 : 1. This can be complicated by those of us who model in 16mm but use 45 mm track to represent wider gauge prototypes such as the Isle of Man Railways.

One may say that, very broadly, G tends to be used by those modelling American or Continental prototypes, and 16 Mill by those of a more parochial turn of mind, to model the British two foot (or thereabouts) gauge railways.

At this stage you may have little idea of what it is you really want or even if your dream specification will fit your pocket book. I will ask you not to concern yourself with these things. There is, after all, plenty of time. Few people, once bitten, voluntarily leave the fraternity of garden railwaymen (or women). There is the rest of one's life to do the job and I would respectfully suggest that the pleasure of research and planning be indulged.

I should here say that this is not a step by step guide to producing a steam railway in your small back yard! One of the strengths of narrow gauge railway modelling in the garden is the rugged individualism of its practitioners and I would hope that this book will provide a framework for you to clothe with your own imagination and ingenuity, to produce a steam railway unique to yourself.

The G Scale Society
Mr A J Day
34 Elgin Avenue
ASHFORD
Middlesex TW15 1QF

The Association of 16mm Narrow Gauge Modellers
Mr E Hodson
Brooklands
Stafford Road
PENKRIDGE
Stafford ST19 5AX

1 Investigating Options

The most difficult part of any project is the start of the beginning. Undefined enthusiasm will eventually settle down to a desire to do something concrete, but where in this bewildering and possibly expensive new world does one start? Of course while motive power tends to occupy centre stage in one's imagination many people will earnestly suggest that you plan and build your railway before considering anything else. Very true, very proper and I'm sure that one should, but I didn't - and what's more I bet you don't!

"I dream of steam trains running through living scenery at my behest." O/K I know the seagull isn't real - it was free though!

I will admit here that I balked at the thought of building a garden railway. The whole thing seemed just too much to take on and, besides, I didn't know how to do it. My personal dream needed sustenance if it wasn't to wither and die so therefore my primary aim was to somehow acquire a steam locomotive and, while it took several months creative accounting, cost cutting and a certain amount of diplomacy, that's just what I did! The railway, I reasoned, would eventually follow.

Now I am a naturally lazy person but this new, shiny and comparatively expensive steam locomotive sitting reproachfully on its shelf, together with my wife's quizzically raised eyebrow, finally spurred me shamefacedly into an orgy of 16mm civil engineering and the Longlands & Western Railway was born.

Luckily my initial enthusiasm had led me to purchase all the back copies of *Sixteen Mill Today* (The house organ of the estimable Association of 16mm Narrow Gauge Modellers). This was, and almost certainly still is, the most extensive archive of narrow

gauge garden railway lore available and certainly prevented this modeller from making some basic, fundamental and enthusiasm sapping errors.

Of course I am not going to suggest you do things the way I did. Certainly it helps to investigate the broader options and attempt to reconcile the parameters of available space and budget with our dream of a private steam railway, but I don't want you to feel guilty at just going ahead and procuring your dream locomotive because that's just what I did! It's worth bearing in mind however, the gentleman who purchased an expensive new Rover motor car only to find that it was too long for his garage! Silly advertisement really, no-one is really that daft......are they?

To view one's railway empire from a comfortable railway bench on a sunny afternoon is a delight. There doesn't have to be a train but I'm sure you have spotted the modified Mamod in the foreground

It's Not the Size that counts...

It cannot be overstressed that one does not need a paddock behind the west wing to get the best from garden railfairing. In fact I would go so far as to say that if one's line is too large then both operating and ongoing maintenance become a chore rather than a pleasure. My Longlands and Western Railway is small but (I would like to think) perfectly formed. My modest back garden has limited me to a space less than 30 feet by 20 and, despite this restriction, the evolution of this little line has provided the scope for many years' pleasurable designing, building and running. In many ways minimum space can be an advantage, cutting on track costs and forcing

A real railway with real steam and real opening doors! *The Reverend,* a Roundhouse Pooter meths fired 0-4-0, has steam to spare during a busy station stop at Harpers Hill

imagination to provide scenic and structural innovation rather than just plain trackwork.

Of course I should like more space, and at some time in the future, when one's offspring are making their way in the world and hopefully keeping their aged parents in luxury, another, larger garden will provide the space for the definitive LWR. It won't however be too large because my hobby, by definition, needs to remain a pleasure.

Compromise

It is politic to involve partner and other family members in this initial exploration of opportunities. The other uses of the garden area have certainly to be considered, more particularly if one's partner is horticulturally minded and mundane practicalities have also to be borne in mind. I spent hours looking out of my window while dreaming and planning, but it was my wife who dryly pointed out the necessity for making arrangements for the washing "whirly". My perfectly reasonable suggestion regarding the front garden for this apparently essential item was not, unfortunately, entertained.

Compromise is the key here and perhaps if not interested in the actual railway, one's other half may be interested in the gardening possibilities specified in later chapters. Gardening skills would of course be very welcome when contemplating rockery and alpine plant cultivation. I would suggest that the application of a certain amount of flattery, together with the seeking of both horticultural and general advice may precipitate a positive reaction and even active involvement!

Simplicity

It may be that you have already started to draw out paper versions of your garden railway empire. Certainly I did many such plans, although most, with their plethora of pointwork and sidings, foundered on the rock of expense. This of course was just as well, because simplicity suits garden railways and bearing in mind that prototype narrow gauge railways were built because they were cheaper, we are conducting our affairs correctly by being sparing with pointwork. My railway started life with five points and has "progressed" to four since closure of the awkward road to the goods shed and cattle dock. Heavy and box freight are now handled from a platform on the old engine shed road and parcels at the platform at Longlands. Plans are in hand for a gated private siding with a tree lined route to our local quarry which will utilise the redundant turnout. But I digress.

Continuous Running

It is suggested that if one has a small garden and is considering running live steam then the availability of a continuous loop is important. It may well not fit the dream - and prototypical operation with one's hand always at the regulator may be envisaged - but make no mistake, there will be occasions when one just wants to sink gratefully into a recliner and watch the trains steam by! It is of course always possible to build a railway that can provide both types of operation and, whatever your motive power, there will come a time when you will bless the possibility of uninterrupted running.

A point rarely considered when doodling plans for a garden railway for the first time is the dimension of height. Now I'm sure that you have taken into account the almost certain premise that your garden is not flat and may even have taken care to postulate cuttings, tunnels and embankments etc. This is all good stuff of course but for me the most important consideration is the height of the railway in the area where steaming, servicing and marshalling of trains is taking place. It may be of course that your lithe young body is perfectly happy bending down to ground level to make some small adjustment or to hook up a three link coupling, but I am doing a racing start for my half century and these days prefer to conduct my pleasures in as much comfort as can be arranged. Every six inches above ground is a bonus and while, because of the slope of the garden the LWR has its share of cutting and tunnelling, working areas are at a comfortable altitude and operations are best viewed from a full size LWR station seat on the hardstanding.

You may well at this initial planning stage already have decided ideas about what type of railway you want. Perhaps a G scale American narrow gauge pike with a radio controlled Roundhouse Sandy River & Rangely Lakes 2-6-2. This would look very attractive hauling a consist of those superb LGB clerestory coaches along elephant proof German metals past the attractively detailed Pola depot. Maybe you would prefer a scarlet liveried Finescale Quarry Hunslet with manual control, piloting a small rake of loaded slate wagons along the two foot gauge, threading its way through the Welsh hinterland.

Freelance

Another option, and perhaps currently the commonest, would be the freelance steam railway. This may employ locomotives with a full size prototype but could equally well take up a generic locomotive as produced by several well known manufactures. The idea of course is primarily to have a steam railway upon which the builder can impress his individual stamp, with exclusive liveries for rolling stock locomotives and structures. This is perhaps one of the attractions of narrow gauge with its accent on the small and self contained. Certainly I regard the Longlands & Western as a real railway, with its own house style and many people even have a full range of paperwork for their line with timetables and tickets etc. I don't go that far, but certainly railway correspondence is conducted on LWR headed notepaper.

Maybe financial considerations preclude any acquisition of steam locomotion at this time, and in later chapters I hope to show how pecuniary constraints can be circumvented to a degree. Just for the moment however, I should like to mention that attractive, effective and pleasurable steam locomotion can be obtained for around two hundred pounds - less than the cost of many 0 gauge white metal locomotive kits.

A flamboyant pair of Finescale Peckett locomotives on Austin Major's line in Suffolk

2 Buying or Acquiring Live Steam

Once upon a time model live steam locomotives were the preserve of either the very affluent or the skilled model engineer. My own perception of live steam was that it was restricted to either "ride behind" or to outstanding examples of engineering excellence with little reference to modelling anything other than motive power. Certainly when my general interest in railways turned specifically to modelling I automatically turned to the table-top scales, largely because I didn't see any other way ahead, but also because I wanted to model railways not just engines! At that time it never occurred to me that it would be possible to actually consider live steam locomotion for my model railway.

Probably most of us who model in the scenic garden scales have arrived by much the same route and most of us are railway modellers rather than engineers. Many folk of course do build their own steam motive power and I have seen some marvellous examples constructed with the basic minimum of tooling. Nevertheless, unless one is already in possession of a full workshop and the necessary skills to make use of it then I would suggest that one's first locomotive at least should be purchased.

There are reasons for this proposal and perhaps the most important is that I learned more from running and modifying my original purchase than from all other sources put together! If one already has the inclination, or discovers a hitherto unknown engineering bent then, as tooling and experience are acquired, there is no reason why one's own locomotive should not take shape at some time in the future. Meanwhile of course, one has the pleasure of building and running a railway with suitable live steam motive power.

Most people then, purchase their steam locomotives, choosing from an ever growing selection of manufacturers and individual builders, who are between them producing models of increasing sophistication and with ever improving standards of reliability.

"Nine years old and long paid for..."
LWR No 2 *Toni*

Financial Considerations

It is at this point that I should like to look this matter of cost squarely in the face! It may be of course, that you do not consider that your current financial position will bear the purchase price of a steam locomotive of whatever type and both loco and railway must remain a dream.

I can't speak for anyone else, but I very definitely remember the utter impossibility of joining the ranks of the home locomotive builders - no matter how comprehensive the instructions, the steamy skills required just seemed way beyond my perceived ability. Equally it appeared inconceivable that I could find the cash to purchase a proper steam locomotive from our very limited family budget. I know of course that many people have faced this particular dilemma and its very true to say that few households are in a position to face spending possibly several hundred pounds on a projected hobby with equanimity.

When I made my first tentative steps towards purchase of a live steam locomotive it was very quickly realised that I had somehow to provide the wherewithal to purchase without affecting the family budget. I therefore decided that I would have to borrow the money and find the repayments by adjusting my personal spending.

Picking up one of those many offers of finance that drop through the letter box once the financial houses realise that (with family and mortgage) one is no longer the feckless waster of yore, it is noted that the cost of a reasonable steam model over three years works out at around £25 per month. Easy to say of course but unfortunately rather more difficult to do. After deciding to proceed I instituted my savings routine for some months before committing myself, to prove, both personally and to my family that I could do it. This period was profitably used to soak up as much information as I could from the model press in general and the back numbers of *Sixteen Mill Today* in particular.

Hence was born my personal mantra of "three pints a week and an evening newspaper" which still funds my hobby today. I did of course buy that first steam locomotive, and the purchase of a radio controlled Merlin Mayflower, complete with steam whistle was eventually accomplished. The smell of steam oil and new paint when I opened the parcel remains an abiding memory, and this much modified little engine, nine years old and long paid for, is still a regular performer on West Country metals. I should also say that spending this not inconsiderable amount so horrified me that my indolent nature was prodded into making a start on the formation of what is now the Longlands & Western Railway!

Note the cab controls in this Finescale locomotive, suitable for 12 inches to the foot fingers

Pre-Purchase Thoughts

It is very difficult indeed to attempt to look at steam locomotives in isolation from other factors which affect our projected steam railway. We have of course already considered the financial aspect but there is much else to be deliberated to ensure a suitable purchase. We may dream of a Pearse Leek & Manifold locomotive or perhaps a DJB Lynton and Barnstaple *Lew* but if our curves are limited to Mamod proportions then that dream will have to be modified. It may be of course that we wish to model an actual railway. If so one would need

A steam Railcar, manufactured by Locomotion of Nuneaton, passing the cafe on the SHLR

to consider availability of rolling stock kits etc, more particularly if one's constructional skills are as yet untested.

Engine Control

A problem seldom mooted but very real nevertheless, is our perception of what is actually on offer! Wishful thinking tends to colour our critical faculties. For instance who wants a locomotive with no apparent means of control? Certainly coming from a background of electrically powered railways, the thought of a manually controlled locomotive seemed to hark back to a dark clockwork past. It certainly seemed to me that radio control was very essential and I had visions of carefree afternoons nonchalantly driving my radio controlled Mayflower on my own private railway. In practice, I found that radio control, as supplied by all manufacturers and builders is not a particularly relaxing way to drive one's locomotive! Experience taught me that the most placid locomotive (as supplied) was a methylated spirit fired, manually controlled pot boiler!!

Having said that of course all my motive power actually is radio controlled, but, except for station stops, shunting and blowing the steam whistle, the radio transmitter is invariably off! The point is that while radio control is an absolute boon, it was not what I perceived it to be. I was at this point already a member of the 16mm Association but I have to say that I felt very diffident about attending a meeting without having a locomotive. It would have helped if I had, because it was really only luck that I purchased something that was suitable for my needs and I would say that my reticence regarding garden meetings was completely unwarranted. Most people that I

A Roundhouse four-coupled "Jack". Reliable modern 16mm steam power (courtesy Roundhouse Engineering)

know in the Association actively welcome new members and certainly I am very happy to hand over the controls of any of my locomotives to anyone who would like to try their hand. Attendance at these events means, at the very least, one can see the locomotives running in a garden environment and discuss them with like-minded individuals.

There is usually, at this stage, a "dream" locomotive. We have seen it advertised in the magazines and may even have read a review of it. We will first of all assume that it is affordable and now need to measure it against other parameters. How user friendly is it for a start? One has of course read the review and the writer would appear to have had no difficulty with the loco so that may be fine of course. Well, I review quite a lot of locomotives and believe me it is very easy to forget that a reader may have no experience at all with model steam engines, or to remember that a minor hitch, nowadays not worth mentioning, would have baffled me a few years ago.

It has to be said that because of this I recently decided not to review a certain engine. I have to say that it was beautifully built; nevertheless, it had taken two experienced steamologists the best part of a couple of days to figure out how it worked. I still like the locomotive but would certainly not wish to recommend it to someone new to the hobby!

I am willing to be challenged on this point but as a general rule the more detailed and accurately scaled a locomotive is the more difficult it is to run. An obvious illustration of this point is the layout of a locomotive cab in 16mm scale, where "twelve inches to the foot" fingers have a problem with a scale regulator handle or reversing lever through the cab door. Compromises have therefore to be made in a garden scale model to improve ergonomics and drivability. Lots of external rivets are fine but tiny and delicate detail parts are not suitable for the rough

A delightful pair of contractors locomotives built by John Prescott of Prescott Engineering and available at a keen price (courtesy J Prescott)

and tumble of running a real steam train in the open air and the major manufacturers are well aware of this.

Detail and Realism

I know this sometimes bothers modellers used to obtaining the highest level of detail possible but realism is approached by different paths in the garden. I well remember running my Merlin Mayflower at a local model engineering exhibition a few years ago. It was easily the simplest locomotive present - not a model of anything in particular - but "Toni", with her ample steam plume, loud chuff, radio controlled steam whistle and pert Victorian demeanour, looked and sounded like something the audience had ridden behind during a trip to Wales. "That's the best one Dad!" did not, I'm afraid, endear me to my fellow exhibitors!

Another important consideration is size and length. This was brought home to me very forcibly when running the DJB Lynton and Barnstaple

This Roundhouse 'Argyll', typical of the larger prototype model, was lined and lettered by Don Arthur for his Tamarside Railway

locomotive. The L&B was really a narrow gauge main line and an accurate model of one of these engines needs a 16mm line built to similar standards. Now I'm quite proud of my Longlands & Western Railway but with its sharp and sometimes checkrailed curves, involuntary gradients and a certain amount of subsidence over the years it has to be said that it is more suited to four coupled locomotives. If your garden is small and you wish to base your line on an actual prototype, then you may wish to consider the Glyn Valley Tramway or the Corris Railway rather than the L&B or the Ffestiniog. One can also have live steam in a very small area by conducting a quarry type operation. Obviously then, available space will have a bearing on our final motive power choice.

Leek & Manifold engine *J B Earle* built by Pearse Locomotives and available from Garden Railway Specialists. It is understood that coaches will be available for this loco. How about the standard gauge transporter waggons?

Firing Small Engines

The commonest general type of steam engine commercially available today has an internally gas fired boiler. The meths fired "pot boiler", so called because it is heated by a heat source under the boiler like a kettle, has become relatively rare from a commercial point of view. They still enjoy a large degree of popularity and certainly have many advantages, such as "silent" firing, simplicity and long duration of run but it cannot be denied that they can be a bit messy. Even with good quality spirit one's shiny brass steam dome quickly becomes discoloured and if a scale model, it is a distinct aesthetic disadvantage to be confined to a black boiler whatever the livery of the rest of the locomotive! Despite this, many locos suit this method of firing and if you can get your hands on a second-hand Roundhouse "Pooter" then think about it very seriously!

Internal gas firing on the other hand, is generally neater, cleaner and more immediately controllable. Modern gas burners are far more silent than of yore and in fact when test running one of Roundhouse Engineering's latest products I had difficulty, at normal running settings, hearing the burner at all! A certain amount of care is required to be exercised with this fuel however. Anyone who has been around small steam engines for any length of time will have witnessed the disconcerting sight of someone fuelling a gas fired engine with a cigarette between their lips! A less obvious example is to see gas fuelling taking place while a meths fired locomotive approaches on an adjacent track! Generally speaking of course, manufacturers react to the market and gas firing is what most people want. It is, in any case, more aesthetically suitable for most types of locomotive produced today.

I haven't of course mentioned internal methylated spirit or coal firing and this is for the very simple reason that I consider a suitable amount of experience is required before attempting to run this type of locomotive. For the same reason I don't intend herein to embark on a technical treatise, no matter how fascinating, on the internal workings of each particular type. The information is widely available and I suggest you will easily find it if you wish to delve into the model engineering aspects of the hobby. Like most modellers I lean toward the romantic aspect of steam locomotion and technical skills have been learnt as they become necessary.

Assuming then, that financial parameters have been met, let us have a look at suitable locomotives on today's market.

The Locomotives

The accent for this first (or only) locomotive is still on the smaller model. I do this because no matter how much space or money is available for motive power there is always room for the switcher, shunter or small working locomotive. In any case the four coupled engine is far more typical of the narrow gauge than a 4-6-0 tender locomotive and we are today fairly spoilt for choice. I cannot here conduct a review of every locomotive on the market but can I hope provide the flavour of what is available.

If you have proceeded far enough in your investigation of garden steam to buy this book you will have heard of Roundhouse Engineering of Doncaster. They produce a range of internally gas fired models and have a well deserved reputation for reliability and logistical back up. Easy to run without losing the individuality indigenous to steam locomotion, their reliability coupled with a comprehensive user manual makes them a popular choice for the newcomer. Currently Roundhouse produce several four coupled models including one with a tender. They have no particular prototype but are based on general types of locomotive. The latest model to date is a delightful continental steam tram engine. *Stanley* has bags of character and would be a pleasure to personalise with full Victorian style lining and lettering.

For those of a more parochial persuasion *Jack* is typical of the British slate or quarry type engine and is also very much at home on small passenger lines. All locomotives in the range are available for both 32mm and 45mm gauge track and may be manually or radio controlled. My personal preference is for radio control of course, because R/C is a comparatively small proportion of the cost and it can always be switched off if one wishes to sit and watch the trains go by.

Another popular manufacturer with a growing reputation for producing fine gas fired locomotives with a respectable level of detail is Pearse

Locomotives of Shropshire. In common with Roundhouse, Pearse are tending to produce larger models of prototype locomotives but they do manufacture a four coupled generic loco of vaguely Hudswell Clarke appearance. *Auric* has a comparatively large boiler and with the addition of a boiler fill system is able to remain in steam all day. With single channel radio control *Auric* is easy to drive and the comprehensive instructions are written with the new driver in mind. I was going to say that all Pearse engines are designed solely for radio control but as these words are put to bed information has reached me about a new locomotive.

Fubero is also a Hudswell Clarke loco, the prototype of which was exported to Mexico. This engine will not be radio controlled but as I understand it a retro fit may well be possible. There will also be a tender available which raises the possibility of gradually upgrading the specification of one's steam motive power.

While Pearse, with the one proposed exception, are wedded to radio control for their family of locomotives, Finescale Engineering do not produce radio controlled models at all. What they do produce is arguably the prettiest range of small four coupled live steam locomotives on the market. These are all beautifully engineered models of actual locomotives, with the Talyllyn's *Dolgoch* as top of the range, but my personal favourite has to be a scarlet quarry Hunslet. Take a look at the Finescale stand at one of the increasing number of garden railway shows around the country and you will see what I mean. These small locomotives are rather more difficult to handle than the products of Pearse or Roundhouse, primarily because of their size and lack of radio control, but if most of your railway is in easy reach they are by no means beyond the skills of the new steamologist.

John Prescott Engineering of Staffordshire is one of the smaller manufactures and produces a very attractive contractors locomotive that runs like a watch. Available in both side and saddle tank versions, Mr Prescott has now added two channel radio control. I enjoyed driving the manual version of this locomotive and was very intrigued at a recent garden railway show, to see how cleverly receiver and servo's have now been shoehorned into this tiny engine.

Most of the models mentioned above fall broadly into the mid price range for steam locomotives - I can't mention them all and of course I haven't tried every locomotive on the market, but today's manufacturers offer well engineered products and it's a matter of matching specification and performance to one's requirements.

Budget Steam Power

I should now like to turn to the section of the market that tends in other areas of endeavour to be labelled "budget". It needs to be stressed that in the world of miniature steam, certain parameters of quality have to remain the same - we are, after all, dealing with pressure vessels here. Nevertheless ingenuity, radical thinking and careful costing have produced several examples of steam motive power at a significantly lower price.

Pride of place in this section currently has to go the meths fired Brandbright *Jane* which is available at around two hundred pounds. The traditional starter model was always the Mamod steam toy with oscillating cylinders but, with the advent of *Jane*, one can acquire a properly engineered model with a high pressure boiler at just a few pounds more. Despite its low price this engine has features usually found on more expensive mainstream locomotives, including a gauge glass so that one can see how much water is in the boiler. New on the market at time of writing, I confidently expect this locomotive to spawn a new hobby of "*Jane* bashing" with special sections in competitions and "How to Do it" articles in the garden railway press!

A particularly interesting model with bags of character at a very good price, is the steam railcar built by Locomotion of Nuneaton. This distinctive vehicle is powered from a vertical gas fired boiler, again using oscillating cylinders. A very smooth runner this railcar may easily be radio controlled. The timber superstructure coupled with the length of the unit means that the receiver can be positioned well away from the moving metal and therefore the cheaper 27meg radios may be employed without fear of radio "glitches". Trailer cars may also be purchased enabling a complete radio controlled steam train to be purchased in stages.

Salem Steam Models, well known for their Mamod modifications, are another company specialising in pushing the "more for less" envelope and currently produce the cheapest locomotive with "proper" reciprocating cylinders. Nicely engineered, the Coal class locomotives are well worth investigation.

Again I haven't mentioned all the manufacturers. Mike Chaney produces some well made meths fired engines at a keen price and Maxwell Hemmens, while being perhaps too expensive for the budget tag, do offer their Ogwen as a bolt together kit for the financially careful and mechanically adroit.

Larger Engines

I have so far carefully restricted this dissertation to four coupled engines which of course excludes *Lady Anne*, the most popular locomotive in terms of numbers, on the market. This Roundhouse model has undergone a long and careful programme of improvement since it first appeared on the market in 1982 and is an excellent choice. One doesn't have to confine one's selection to small engines. Locomotives like *Lady Anne* or the Pearse *Genesis* are generic models that are a pleasure to drive. With their close coupled drivers and large boilers, this type of engine is designed to cope with a broad range of track conditions and user skills.

My suggestion that a small model might make a better first choice is just an opinion - not mandatory, and of course if one is modelling a G scale American line then starting small would be pretty difficult! A large model of an actual locomotive, if one has the financial resources and the space, will provide a lot of pleasure. My only reservation here, is that it would be desirable to purchase this first locomotive from a manufacturer with a track record of producing models that are easy to run. If one has to have a large prototypical model then for example, a Pearse *Countess* or Roundhouse *Argyll* are carefully designed to provide a fairly detailed model that is comparatively easy to use.

Whatever ones choice it is not completely irrevocable. Please bear in mind that steam engines from a well known builder hold their price pretty well, and if after experience, one wishes to look at something a little more complicated then one can always resell which brings me neatly to:

Second-hand Engines

I believe the latest term from the USA in the automobile trade is "pre-owned". I think its supposed to sound comfortable and safe. Nevertheless an appropriate expression for the novitiate steamologist is *caveat emptor*. One would not buy a second hand motorcar from an individual without knowing anything about road vehicles. Equally it would be just as foolhardy to rush into purchase of a comparatively expensive "pre-owned" model without assistance from a more experienced ferrinequinologist. Certainly there are bargains to be had, particularly with older less fashionable models and if one is prepared to do a bit of work this can be seen as a cheap way in. Again, membership of the 16mm Association or G scale Society, would give access to the combined experience of local members and may also locate a local vendor as a member decides to "trade up" to more sophisticated motive power.

Overall, modern steam motive power in the scenic scales is well constructed and reliable. Well known manufacturers provide guarantees, well written user documentation and logistical back up. Nevertheless if one is not in a position to visit a local line then see your purchase steaming! This applies to new as well as second-hand locomotives. I should stress that this is not because a manufacturer is likely to off-load a lemon - but because watching someone service and drive an engine is worth a dozen manuals!

Start saving and have fun!

A Pearse four-coupled generic locomotive on test at Longlands

3
Raising the Pressure

I have noticed over the years how electronic controllers have gradually become more and more sophisticated, allowing the railway modeller to simulate coasting, braking, mass and even to operate an on board whistle or diesel klaxon. Certainly in the garden LGB and various American manufacturers have been at the forefront of this development and, despite my predilection for live steam I have been quite impressed with what has been achieved.

We know of course that no matter what can be accomplished with electronic wizardry it cannot be compared to the real thing. Even our comparatively tiny steam locomotives react in the same way as their full size counterparts and, with regulator handle, reversing lever and steam whistle controlled from afar, we can indulge in a spot of real driving - albeit in miniature.

Perhaps then, you would like to join me in a steaming session both on the Longlands and Western Railway and the South Hams Light Railway, using two very different steam engines for motive power.

Preparation

Before steaming one of the resident engines I have to "walk my length". Rather a grand term for the small LWR in fact because it is the work of a few moments to check around the track for any impediments to running. A small precaution but necessary. I did hear of an unfortunate garden railwayman who neglected to do this and discovered, too late, that a dog had left his calling card on the main line. The resulting collision, involving a hot steam locomotive, did not cause any damage but managed to spoil the owner's whole day!

There is little else to do to prepare the railway for the afternoon train

Topping up the boiler. This engine may remain in steam all day using the boiler fill system

service. I take pride in the fact that my LWR is a real railway and all buildings, signalling and general infrastructure stays in the weather the year round. My only concession to the real world is that the bridge over the River Lyner, in reality, is spanning the garden path and needs to be removable to allow access to the washing whirly!

Of course we will need some stock to pull and the usual LWR mixed train, consisting of four bogie vehicles, is waiting alongside the platform at Longlands station.

Our first engine is a model of the Welshpool and Llanfair "Countess", a nicely detailed product from the Pearse Locomotives stable. Internally gas fired with twin channel radio control, "Countess" is a careful combination of showcase good looks and practical runnability. My model, named *Sir Edward Tapper* after an old friend, is lined and lettered for my Longlands & Western Railway and waits patiently in the servicing section of Longlands yard. This part of the line is alongside the hard-standing, around eighteen inches off the ground and a fairly comfortable working height for me.

Servicing

Preparing a locomotive for running is fairly straightforward and items required for steaming are usually kept together in a small box. The first job

Filling the hydrostatic lubricator in the cab. The steam turret is in the front of the cab and just behind can be seen the steam stop valve and boiler drain wheel. Note the gas filler valve and tap on the port side. All these controls are easy to reach while the locomotive is in steam.

is to check both servo and transmitter batteries. Fairly obvious I know and one would obviously have them charged ready for use - but I have before now accidentally left one or the other switched on and not discovered this until the loco was ready to move - so check anyway!

The locomotive needs to be oiled, watered and fuelled - not necessarily in that order. In fact I always gas my engines up first to enable any butane spillage to disperse before lighting the burner. You will note from the photographs that the cab roof has been removed from the locomotive for servicing. This is my own alteration, in fact on this and most other modern engines the cab roof usually hinges to the front or side. In any case on *Sir Edward* all the servicing arrangements are in the cab. Gassing up is a simple operation. One needs to ensure that the gas valve on the burner is turned off and the canister is held on to the filler valve until the tank is full and the valve vents from the side. The boiler is initially filled via the steam riser/filler turret in the cab using a large syringe. This is of course supplied with your locomotive, but replacements are obtainable from suppliers such as Brandbright, Garden Railway Specialists etc.

You can get them from Boots but one usually has to undergo a grilling from a suspicious pharmacist before they will hand one over - though what else they think one is going to get up to with a syringe this size beggars the imagination!! Its best to use distilled water for your boiler and if you have a dehumidifier this will provide a useful source. Don't worry about overfilling the boiler - before lighting the burner we will open the boiler level valve.

The next job is to fill the lubricator. This is located in the right hand side of the cab tucked behind the side sheet. It has a large screwdriver slot in the knurled cap but, in common with all other fittings it is just finger tight. No tools are required for preparation at all. Fill the lubricator with proper steam oil to the top of the cross member and replace the cap. This is simple and you will have used about two pence worth of oil. I make this point because it amazes me that people will readily pay upwards of a thousand pounds for a top quality model and then try and save on oil! Steam oil is cheap, easily obtainable and if you don't use it you will damage your locomotive. Motor or machine oil will emulsify to uselessness in the temperature obtained in steam cylinders.

Sir Edward is now ready for firing. The gas valve is opened, a lighter applied to the top of the chimney and the flame will "pop" back into the burner tube in the boiler. After a moment for the jet to warm, the gas valve can be turned up and we wait while *Sir Edward* raises pressure.

I quite enjoy these few moments sitting by a locomotive which is slowly coming to life. The time may be usefully employed by oiling round the motion, and this time we can use machine or light motor oil. After a couple of minutes we notice water coming from the boiler drain pipe. You will of course recall that we left the boiler level valve open and as soon as the water stops and steam issues forth we can close the valve wheel in the cab.

On this loco, in common with all Pearse engines, the fittings are all "cool touch" so again, no tools are needed and all user parts are finger friendly.

A glance through the window in the back-sheet, or through the cab door and we note that the pressure gauge is reading about forty pounds. Now the factory given working pressure for this locomotive is between forty and fifty pounds and the safety valve will blow at the latter. In practice this beautifully efficient engine will pull a heavy train with less than twenty pounds on the clock so we have power to spare. We turn down the gas burner to the steady hum of its working setting, switch on both locomotive servos and the radio control transmitter and we are ready to drive the locomotive.

Looking back on the above it does seem more complicated than just putting an electric locomotive on the track and driving off doesn't it? Well I suppose it is, but you see to most of us, the few minutes of preparation with live steam are as pleasurable as driving and I have to say, infinitely preferable to the mundane and backbreaking chore of track cleaning prior to running. I've never had to do this of course, so maybe its fun - but I somehow doubt it!

Driving your Steam Engine

Sir Edward is burbling quietly to himself and so we move the transmitter lever to put the engine into forward gear. A couple of blips on the whistle to clear the pipes, warm up the whistle and of course to follow prototype practice, and we open the regulator. There is little in the way of condensate in the cylinders because we used the boiler level valve during firing and the locomotive moves of down the yard at around scale walking pace. Points are changed and the locomotive moves out onto the main line and pauses on the Lyner bridge.

The road is set again, the reverser operated and with a blast of the whistle the locomotive moves sedately back into the platform road, kissing buffers with its train. After hooking up the three link coupling with my home made shunter's pole, *Sir Edward* is ready to take the afternoon "mixed" to Saltash Junction. It's a funny thing with small steam engines and part of their charm that while most recent models are relatively easy to drive straight from the factory, there is always a new level of skill to acquire. One *can* charge along the track with the safety valve blowing or of course one can attempt to drive at the generally accepted narrow gauge speed of a scale 15 mph. I happen to enjoy doing the latter. The burner is turned down and I try to make the best use of steam that I can. The exit from Longlands station can be particularly difficult at slow speed with a curve right after the Lyner bridge together with the rising gradient of Trematon Bank to be negotiated and it certainly helps to know the road.

The reverser is put into forward gear and with a blast of the steam whistle we allow steam into the cylinders. Careful now because we don't wish to go charging unprototypically down the main line! Our steed responds well to an experienced driver and the connecting rods start to move as the train is eased away from the platform and rumbles over the Lyner Bridge. Passing through a small wood with a brick built permanent way hut on our right it's time to open the regulator for the ascent of Trematon Bank.

This is perhaps my favourite part of the line and one that I try to negotiate as slowly as possible. The exhaust sharpens as the engine works hard to maintain headway, one can hear each individual beat of the locomotive and on a calm day the steam drifts through the trees creating an aural and visual picture that is, to me, wholly delightful. At the top of the bank we rumble over a gated level crossing into the small hamlet of Trematon. Trains stop here as required, but proceeding slowly from our exertions on the bank it's easy to see that no business awaits this afternoon and we plunge into the cool depths of Trematon Tunnel before emerging into the dank and tree lined cutting.

Coasting down the Grade

At this point we are on a downgrade and so the regulator is eased back allowing Sir Edward to coast quietly along. A warning board informs us of the horrendous check railed curve below the footbridge to Trehan Chapel and accordingly, the regulator is almost closed. Unfortunately dictated by the topography of the garden, this curve is set in deep tree hung cutting and drivers without route knowledge may easily come to grief. The line between

The simple but efficient cab arrangement of Brandbright's *Jane*. Note the water level gauge glass - this will add immeasurably to your running pleasure. You will have spotted the lubricator in the cab and the boiler filler valve is, of course, atop the boiler. This is another locomotive that will remain in steam continuously

imagination and reality is very close but one of the practicalities of negotiating this section of track is that one is dependent on the sound of the train and the position of the steam plume. As the flanges bite into the curve, experienced operators will open the regulator for steady acceleration to negotiate this and the following reverse curve. For this reason Trehan footbridge is a favourite place for photographers - locomotives are generally working very hard and producing a sharp exhaust with lots of steam.

We need to maintain plenty of steam to the cylinders as we pass the now disused goods shed with its rusting and weed covered spur and upon reaching the timber framed water tower the regulator is almost closed to coast smoothly into the platform road of Longlands station.

Trains and Boats and Planes

It is here that newcomers to the regulator handle, perhaps used to the direct response of a motor car, tend to throw our 16mm passengers to the floor. I have always considered driving a steam locomotive to be rather more akin to controlling a boat or an aeroplane rather a car. We are not here increasing the direct drive of an electric motor, but instead controlling the amount of steam available to the power source of an unbraked vehicle. Response is therefore neither direct or instant. Some people grasp this instinctively - others need time and practice.

After around twenty five minutes running the train is left in the platform road while the loco moves back to the yard and my servicing point for replenishment. Using the boiler fill system *Sir Edward* may be watered and oiled whilst in steam. In fact I generally recharge the lubricator every hour and top up the boiler every twenty minutes or so whilst running and this engine can steam happily along all day. Do be aware however, that the gas burner MUST be turned off before recharging the gas tank.

Sir Edward Tapper then, simmers quietly on a spur in the autumnal sunshine, gas turned right down awaiting a call to duty. This afternoon, running powers are conferred to visiting motive power and the pride of the line is regulated to the job of "stand-by locomotive" and yard shunter, preparing trains for visitors. I can hear the latch on the garden gate and so its time to welcome my guests with a cup of tea...

Meths Fired "Pot Boiler"

Our next locomotive is rather a different proposition. At less than a fifth of the price of *Sir Edward* one might be forgiven for thinking that the pleasure obtained may be proportionally less. I have to say that this is not the case and I found the Brandbright/IP Engineering locomotive *Jane* to be one of the most entertaining little engines that I have ever driven.

It is different of course. Here we have an externally meths fired locomotive with oscillating cylinders and boasting no particular prototype. Nevertheless she is a pretty little engine which captures the look of those early Victorian four coupled narrow gauge locomotives such as those produced by George England. No radio control of course but very tractable and possessing a boiler fill system coupled with a water level sight glass. This last is something that even *Sir Edward* cannot boast and *Jane* can be kept continuously in steam , even by the most inexperienced steamologist.

Preparation

We raise steam in the South Hams Light Railway steaming bay, filling the boiler first using the ""Hoselock" bottle standard on these boiler fill systems. Note the level rising on the gauge glass as this operation takes place. The displacement lubricator on this engine is also tucked behind the side-sheet and is filled to the cross member in the same way as *Sir Edward.* The meths fuel tank is simply charged by means of a syringe taking care not to cause any spillage. It does not do to be too cavalier with procuring spirit for this purpose. That which is sold in hardware shops tends to be recovered from all sorts of unmentionable sources and, apart from having a lower heat coefficient, will very quickly make your new locomotive very dirty. Methylated spirit BP is the stuff we want and if you buy it at the same time as your large syringe you will really spook the pharmacist!!

Jane is of course externally fired and in common with other locos of this type has the wicks enclosed in a very neat weatherproof firebox. Actually getting at the wicks to light them can be difficult and most owners construct a special bay or rig to enable this operation to be conducted easily. The bay on the SHLR is purpose built with an angled mirror under the track so one can confirm that all wicks are lit.

As before we can oil round the locomotive to ensure everything is as it should be while steam is raised. *Jane* has no pressure gauge and the safety valve will start to pass wisps of steam as pressure is reached. We don't of course have to faff around with fancy radio systems and batteries so as pressure is reached we can put the reverser into forward gear and open the regulator.

Hands on the Regulator

This is a very controllable locomotive - it won't rush away but will start to move according to pressure and regulator setting. As the new steamologist concerns himself with the business of collecting his train, confidence in *Jane* will very quickly be gained. It is perfectly possible to back the locomotive onto its train with no unseemly crashing of buffers and after hooking up our three link coupling we can be on our way. No whistle I'm afraid but then not everyone shares my obsession with the things and the biggest manufacturer of "scenic scale" engines in the world does not fit them at all.

With the few seconds pause the locomotive's safety valve is blowing again and it is time to open the regulator - bearing in mind that we are no longer "light engine"- and Jane takes the train out onto the main line.

Graham Wilkins' SHLR has sweeping curves and is easily accessible for almost all its length - ideal conditions for a manually controlled engine. We therefore set the regulator for a reasonable scale speed and sit down with our cup of Earl Grey (they do things properly on the South Hams line) to enjoy the sight and sound of our train chuffing busily into the middle distance.

Watching the Trains go by

It is a simple matter, as the train sweeps sedately round the tea shop curve, to cock an eye to the gauge glass and adjust the regulator if required. Twenty minutes later with the gauge glass dropping we can top up the boiler and fuel tank and send the train on its way. In common with her more expensive shed mate the lubricator will need charging every hour otherwise there is no reason why this well built little locomotive should not steam along continuously for as long as you wish. This is relaxing, just sitting by the lineside with a steam train passing every two or three minutes - tea, biscuits and railway chat on a sunny summer afternoon.

Back to the Shed

At the end of the day's steaming and in common with twelve inches to the foot scale a certain amount of work is required - although in our case a wipe over with a clean cloth while the engine is still warm will suffice. The probability is however, that like myself, you will enjoy cleaning your locomotive and fussing with your brass dome. My engines are cleaned, polished and on display, giving pleasure even when cold and immobile.

I hope that the above has given the flavour of steam running in your garden because it's now time to look at the more mundane practicalities of building one's garden railway.

This manually controlled little locomotive is very tractable and with its open cab is ideal for shunting operations. *Jane* makes up her train at Harpers Hill

4
Dreaming into Action

The probability is that at this stage there will have been several proposed garden layouts. If one has a neat and ordered mind, these will have been committed to paper after due consideration and consultation with the other users of the garden. If, on the other hand, one depends like myself on a vague scenario formed from hours spent gazing at the allotted plot of land, one's action plan will remain in the imagination, to be drawn out and polished perhaps, during odd moments in the working day.

Of course I really don't think it matters too much which way we approach the problem, but there are however a few points that you may find useful at this stage.

First of all we need to take into account our motive power. I am of course assuming that it will be live steam and it is suggested that your railway is as level as can be achieved. This is not because a steam locomotive cannot handle gradients. With the possible exception of the Mamod, they all can, with varying degrees of ease. No, the reason is that you will get them anyway, and in a small garden the locomotive may be taking a check-railed curve as part of the train is on a carefully planned gradient! Fine with radio control but a manual steam locomotive or a light diesel may be more work than pleasure on this type of line. Despite my efforts I certainly have gradients on the LWR - and I can assure you that they were not planned!

Is it the intention to run large radio controlled locomotives pulling lengthy trains - or perhaps a small manual quarry locomotive bumbling round the

Tunnels - A blistering nuisance? Maybe so, but they add to the general railway atmosphere and in any case, just like mine, they are sometimes necessary. *Thomas Alfred* makes a fine sight bursting out from the portal

garden with half a dozen slate wagons? Now I would suggest that if at all possible then your line should be able to accommodate every likely sort of motive power within the constraints of available space. The reason for this is very simply because garden railfaring is, above all, a sociable hobby and one quickly finds that enjoyment of one's steam railway is enhanced by sharing it with like-minded people - who will of course, bring engines of their own.

Some people create what I call an outdoor "indoor" railway using bench-work. Nothing wrong with that of course and in some gardens it seems the only way to get a decent amount of height, more particularly if one finds bending is a problem. Timber construction does however, have to be fairly massive to cope with the vagaries of the British climate and scenic possibilities are limited.

Civil Engineering

On a personal level I prefer the ethos of the real thing in miniature, with trains running through living scenery, and a happier solution, for me, is to is to have a ground level line with a raised area to facilitate servicing of locomotives. This is easier than it might first appear. Very few gardens are completely level and my small plot slopes gently from the back fence towards the house. The railway therefore passes through most types of civil engineering structures and earth-works as it circumnavigates the garden, with the main station area both a couple of feet from the ground and convenient to the tea making facilities!

Many people construct their line on or between dwarf walls. This is a method of construction that I am particularly fond of because it provides a singularly stable trackbed at a suitable height for both watching and servicing of trains. George Mckie's Plymstock and Hooe Light Railway is an example of this genre. The track bed itself is of concrete block construction with stone facings. A key point in the line's design is that, while all areas of the railway are accessible from the front, structures and plantings can be placed behind the railway. Rockeries will add to the interest and I would pile it high, filling pockets with horticultural grit together with peat for alpine plants and miniature conifers to thrive. Bear in mind that stone is always "in scale" - that's why the Japanese use it to display bonsai trees to best effect!

While it is probably obvious that manual engines would require a reasonable amount of lineside access, it is of course no bad thing for any locomotive. Running out of gas in one of the more inaccessible corners of the railway empire is a traditional minor misjudgement but with a bit of forward planning need not result in an undignified scramble over the flower beds. The Longlands & Western has simple gravel paths providing entry to almost all sections of the line and most garden railways allow a reasonable level of approachability.

It is this problem with accessibility that has led many pundits to regard tunnels as a blistering nuisance. I must confess to a pang of disappointment when I came across this opinion for the first time - primarily because I like tunnels, cuttings, bridges and embankments! All these civil engineering features combine to add character and life to our endeavours and my own tunnel is in any case a necessary formation to allow the permanent way to negotiate the garden path. So by all means indulge in a tunnel or two if this is your wish, but it is suggested that it extends for considerably less than two arms lengths. Even this distance is slightly problematical, as anyone who has tried to extricate a hot and spitting live steamer from their optimistic excavations will tell you. Perhaps just long enough to provide a scenic feature is the way ahead.

Cuttings of course go together with tunnels and can also cause problems. A derailment below ground level for instance, is difficult to deal with if one is not over-fond of bending. Leaves on the line regularly cause high profile difficulties for Network South East but at least they don't have to deal with a whole cutting full at a time! Nevertheless, if like me you enjoy seeing a column of steam marching along the countryside before the train hoves into view, you will probably contemplate cuttings. In any case unless your garden is billiard table flat you will probably require both cutting and embankment.

Now the problem with embankments is that they are by definition "made ground" and therefore subject to subsidence. In many cases however our line is likely to be cut into the side of a slope or built on the edge of a rockery rather than a stand alone embankment.

Bridges

I have never had any sort of difficulty with bridges. While they are quite expensive to purchase they are cheap and comparatively simple to scratch build. We will later look at bridge building but at this stage its worth investigating a likely location for this structure. As with indoor layouts we have a certain amount of control over our topography and we will wish our civil engineering features to look at home in the landscape.

Having negotiated a vague right-of-way it's therefore time to sit and look at all the various options scribbled on the back of the proverbial cigarette packet and it is now that we can inject a certain amount of realism into our plans. I have already mentioned the high cost of point-work and the necessity for following the prototype by keeping it to a minimum. It may be of course that both financial and space considerations are not a problem but even so there is a lot to be said for starting small.

One reason is that after a considerable amount of work one might well be unhappy with the basic concept but the single most important factor is human nature. Now you may have the will-power to start a major project and carry it through to completion, to slog through the mud and hump

A rock lined cutting on the Tamarside railway. Visiting engine *Sir Edward Tapper* takes a heavy train through the reverse curve. Note the drainage channels either side of the trackbed

concrete blocks in the sure and certain knowledge that you will be running trains along a magnificent railway in eighteen months time, but I'm afraid that I have to take things in small bites with easily achievable targets to get anything done at all.

I could also quote without shame the dictum of a certain Peter Jones who advocates "getting something running". Therefore, if your railway is going to be a complicated and heavily engineered affair with branches in all directions, may I suggest that you consider phasing your operations to provide an initial simple running line that can be enlarged and improved. Believe me, seeing a steam train moving on your own tracks will provide a fillip to your endeavours and kick-start your flagging enthusiasm.

Visitors and Visiting

I have already mentioned the necessity for a convenient area for steaming engines and making up trains. Hopefully at a reasonable height, this part of the railway merits careful planning. Don't forget that you will almost certainly be coping with visitors who may or may not have their own stock with them. Certainly a garden meeting will mean a plethora of locomotive

A masterpiece of engineering on the Tamarside railway. This impressive structure, built of aluminium angle, folds down in the manner of a a washing whirly to allow access without bending

and stock boxes which will need a convenient stowage. Visitors of a non railway minded nature are also often intrigued with the idea of real miniature steam trains running through the rockery and somewhere for them to sit and view operations in comfort needs to be considered.

It's worth saying at this point that any experience with indoor table-top railways is certainly not wasted. You will certainly remember using your imagination when designing your custom made landscapes to provide viewing areas with "scenic breaks" and carefully constructed dioramas. We can do this in the garden as well - the only difference is that our constructional and scenic materials are more elemental. This is the area where brute civil engineering combines uneasily with art and it is something to be contemplated when staring out of the window on a wet and windy Sunday afternoon.

I have already mentioned the possibility of visiting other 16mm or G scale garden railways in your area. This was primarily to see and hopefully try small scale live steam but one can also incorporate good ideas into one's own railway and I have to say that it is also very useful to let other people make the mistakes for you! When I first embarked on this garden railway adventure there were no other lines within easy striking distance and, despite information culled from various sources, the Longlands & Western has had to live with my initial blunders. Later local lines have taken into account the constructional problems I encountered and are the better for it.

Animals, Kids and Vandals

In most cases our garden environment has to be shared with the rest of the family. Now in many ways I was lucky in this respect, because the LWR was constructed after our progeny were both dry in the sump and more interested in girls than playing in the garden. There are no boisterous dogs to rampage along the trackwork destroying buildings and structures - only a single elderly cat who, while she may snooze quietly on the platform in the summer sun, picks her way fastidiously around the infrastructure causing no damage at all. Do not despair if you have an overabundance of small children and/or large dogs. One can of course put buildings out on the line only when running trains but, for me, this destroys the concept of the real garden railway. After all, one would wish to enjoy the line in all its climatic moods, whether trains are running or not. All it means really is that we need to build rather more solid structures capable of surviving a direct hit with a large ball and this will be discussed in a later chapter.

An impressive home built timber trestle, removable for lawn mowing

Before we start on construction I should mention something that I know bothers a lot of people, and that is the spectre of vandalism. Now I have a small back garden with a path which leads from our comprehensive school close by to the local Spar shop and various estates. Moreover the existence of the railway was fairly well known to the younger population via my teenage sons and their friends but has nevertheless been untroubled these ten years.

I do have a six foot fence at the rear and even when the back gate is opened the trees are positioned to screen the railway structures to the casual eye. In any case one cannot let the actions of the mindless minority control one's activities but I do think that the problem is more perceived than real. Perhaps we should get started.

5
Working on the Railroad

All of us of whatever scale or gauge - on indoor or outdoor lines, have one primary problem, and that is of course getting started! Certainly, for several years, the term "armchair modeller" caused me to shift guiltily in my own fireside perch, as I perused the sterling efforts of others in the model railway press. I did plead, with some justification, lack of space but it wasn't until my interest had been engaged by live steam and the possibility of using the garden for my railway activities, that starting a layout was actually contemplated.

We all generally know where to start on an indoor model railway because, before construction of the line, we have to build an artificial terrain through which our trains will run. Base boards or bench-work will therefore be the basis of our model.

I chose the title "Working on the Railroad" for this chapter, because that is what we do in the garden. The Ffestiniog deviation and my Longlands and Western are both narrow gauge railways driven through virgin territory. The difference is merely a matter of scale and gauge. LWR cuttings were carved from earth and shale with a pickaxe and a tunnel was built of shuttered concrete. Embankments were raised using spoil from cuttings and retaining walls were erected before the trackbed was levelled and graded to receive the line. Sounds terribly hard work doesn't it? In fact I consider it simpler than constructing bench-work but that, no doubt, is a matter of perception.

Trackbed

This matter of trackbed construction is one that causes more discussion and controversy than any other aspect of garden railways and conflicting advice coupled with a very natural desire to reduce the perceived amount of work

Early days on the South Hams line at Dartington. Note the concrete block construction

required to get a train running, will often seduce the apprentice garden railwayman into taking short-cuts. One often sees a lightly laid line of fairly recent construction in the model railway press, together with the author's assertion that despite gloomy predictions from various Jeremiahs, no problems have been encountered.

I feel obliged to say that almost certainly the line will not have weathered many winters. Even in the United Kingdom there are quite wide variations of climatic conditions which will affect one's civil engineering works in different ways. Here in the comparatively mild but generally soggy West Country, I rarely encounter such things as "frost heave" but outside woodwork certainly needs to be well protected. The winter of 95/96 provided some fairly fierce weather further north however and I understand Glasgow obtained some twenty degrees below. What that would do to a lightly laid garden railway I don't know!

I know that this will not please some people but my suggestion is that one undertakes the heaviest construction that is practicable. Of course if one's lifestyle dictates that regular house moves are on the cards or perhaps physical disability or financial considerations constrain us then we have to do the best we can.

This assertion is based on hard experience. Part of the trackbed of the

An elderly Merlin wheezes past a permanent way hut. The bare concrete block has now been neatly faced with timber paling

current Longlands and Western Railway was cut through heavy shale with a pick-axe. I started this operation in the heat of the summer and the alliterative name my wife called me - starting with "Silly......." was certainly accurate. It was very hard work indeed. Nevertheless this section of permanent way has caused no problem in ten years. The skimped foundations on the raised section of the railway on the other hand, have been a source of very many hours remedial work and there is the prospect of more to come unless I take the bull by the horns and re-do from scratch.

Surveying and Leveling

The temptation for me was to grab a pickaxe and start digging and, frankly, that's just what I did! I levelled the line pretty well after hacking my route through the scrubland that was my back garden - but it was very much rule of thumb. A long piece of timber lashed to a small spirit level measuring from brick to brick was not the most effective way of ensuring a level track bed and, quite apart from subsequent subsidence, left me with the fierce gradient of Trematon bank. Yes - well I know I said it was my favourite part of the line, but coupled with necessarily sharp curves it has made running on the LWR a bit of an art and visiting drivers need a route knowledge turn before a running session.

What I should have done of course, after roughly excavating the cutting, was to conduct a survey using levelling pegs to get an absolutely flat datum. It is just possible, in a small garden, to undertake this using a spirit level taped to long piece of timber, but if you do decide on this course of action may I recommend using a scaffold pole. This, apparently, is more likely to provide a straight datum than timber - although please don't ask me where you would get one from!

Perhaps the best approach is the tried and tested hose-pipe and lemonade bottle method. Based on the fact that water will find its own level this is a simple way of obtaining a log distance datum and I hope you will find the diagram is self explanatory. I should take the newly dug cutting as a starting point and using the hose-pipe based jury rig, its a good idea to put the second level peg at the point on the proposed line the furthest distance away before "half and halfing" our way back to the starting point.

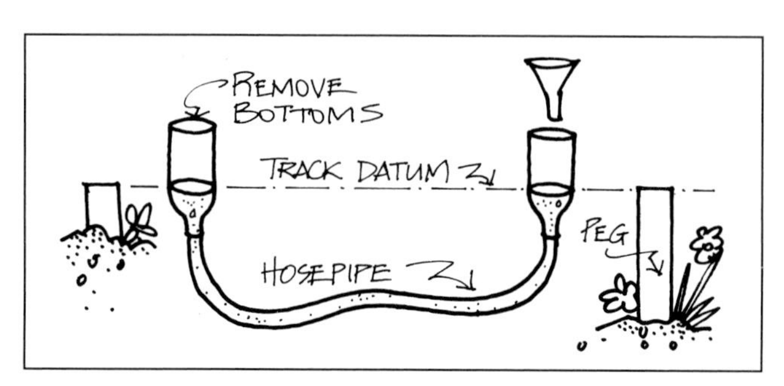

After setting level pegs to mark out the route, I would respectfully suggest that the most heavily constructed track bed that one can manage is the way forward. Digging down to allow consolidated hard-core topped with a sort of dwarf wall would be my ideal. Shuttered concrete on top of the foundation will provide a solid track bed in areas where the route runs at ground level and block-work using any of the commercially available building materials would be suitable for route sections that are above ground. One doesn't have to spend a lot of money on this and I have found old fire bricks from redundant night storage heaters and recovered breeze blocks to be a suitable medium. I know that this type of material isn't particularly attractive but, as you will see, we can either face it with quarry stone or build up rockery to cover this utilitarian structure.

It is important that station and servicing areas are at a comfortable working height. Around two feet is comfortable to use for most people and because of the increased width required at these points it's worth considering the use of paving slabs. These will provide a flat surface and if the space underneath is left clear it will make an ideal stowage for running equipment and visitor's boxes.

If like myself you have a background of indoor model railways, I could perhaps liken this type of construction to that of the "open baseboard" type where the trackbed consists of supported strips on an open frame and the rest of the "scenery" is constructed after this is complete, rather than the solid type baseboard with the trackbed of necessity at the lowest level. We can do something very similar in the garden and our topography can be built up or scooped away from our solid right-of-way.

Embankments and Cuttings

It may be that an embankment is a necessity or perhaps you just wish to have one as a feature and really there is no reason why you shouldn't. Please however bear in mind that this is "made ground", very subject to subsidence and I would suggest that the idea of a dwarf wall is continued. Consolidate your foundation below the original ground level and build up with blocks - not forgetting to leave a hole for an under-bridge if required. If you propose to have an earth embankment don't forget to include lumps of stone leavened with horticultural grit as an anchor for future conifers and alpine plants. This earth embankment will subside and you will need to add material to it until it settles. I understand that the Great Central Railway had similar problems with the grand embankments marching across the Chilterns. Initial GCR services operated under speed restrictions until natural settlement had taken place, but your trains will pass happily over your embankment without inhibition, secure on their dwarf wall base.

Generally speaking the right-of-way in cutting is already on consolidated ground and minimal foundations are required for a solid track-bed. Drainage is particularly important below ground level however and we need to consider possible land slip. Sloping dry stone or mortared wall construction will take care of landslip problems and a bit of forethought will provide small earth pockets to "start" creeping alpine plants. On the

Longlands & Western Railway I employed recovered slates to line my cutting. This worked tolerably well, but an unforeseen problem was that the flat slate in some way interfered with radio signals from my transmitters. Whatever method is chosen it's worth bearing in mind that even on the best run railways the occasional derailment will occur - perhaps a wind blown twig jamming in the track. In any event the cutting will need to be wide enough to re-rail a bogie coach without too much strain.

Our right of way is designed to be flat so it's rather difficult to make arrangements for water to run out of cuttings. Again we

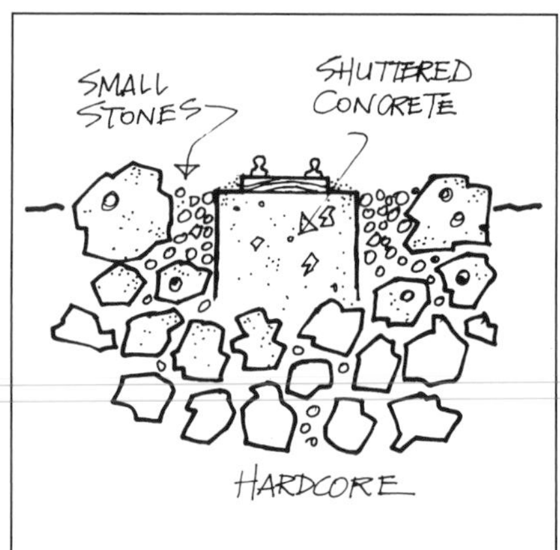

A solid timber baulk track bed on the Silverton and Western Railway. Note the simple timber-built bridge

have to turn to the prototype for inspiration and use a shouldered profile track base with gravel filled drainage culverts either side. Sounds very technical I know but the drawing should make this clear and experience tells me that it works.

Tunnels

The beté noir of garden railway constructors has to be the tunnel. Many well known exponents of garden railway lore will recommend that they are avoided at all costs and unsatisfactory substitutes such as routing the line through a thick bush are suggested. I do see their point of view but to me a tunnel is an essential feature of the railway scene. Indoor lines of course use them as a useful scenic break. While we don't have a fiddle yard to hide it is worth taking into consideration the aesthetic qualities of our endeavours and I have tried to design my small railway as a series of dioramic views. We are constructing the bare bones of our four dimensional artwork and imagination is at least as important as civil engineering at this stage.

I shall take it as read then that a tunnel will be required for your embryo railway and so first of all need to look at some common mistakes. The one that you have all thought of is of course - length! It's fairly easy to see that if one has a derailment in the middle of a six foot tunnel, particularly when employing steam locomotion, then there are all the ingredients for a very expensive disaster! A tunnel then will need its extent restricted to comfortably less than two arms' lengths and it is suggested that it is sited on straight and level track. One can of course get away with a gentle curve and the topography of your garden might, like mine, dictate this.

A tunnel also needs internal dimensions sufficient to pass any locomotive or stock likely to run on the railway. Blindingly obvious one might think - however if one is used to the size ratio of rolling stock to track employed by standard gauge railways then this is a very simple mistake to make and one that you will come across again later in this book. Narrow gauge equipment on the two foot gauge has a considerable overhang particularly on curves, and while I conscientiously checked the throw of my Merlin Locomotive and stock I found that a Roundhouse *Lady Anne* with its extra length, clipped the coping stone of my tunnel mouth and remedial work had to be conducted with a hammer and chisel! Do please bear in mind the height difference between a cabless Welsh quarry locomotive with its train of wagons and an American Mogul with large bogie box cars!

While considering this difference between narrow and standard gauge I am bound to say that it is easy to make this same mistake with passing loops and in station areas. If one is used to standard gauge ratios then it is very easy to place parallel tracks too close together. My 32mm gauge track is at six and a half inch centres which is by no means excessive and its probably best to offer up one's stock and motive power before making a decision. If it is intended to run smaller prototypes do remember that one may wish to entertain visitors who may bring something continental with twelve wheels!!

There are various methods of construction that may be employed to build a tunnel and perhaps the first that comes to mind is a length of large diameter pipe. I'm sure that you will use your ingenuity and whatever materials come to hand, but my tunnel was under the garden path so among other things had to support the weight of a heavy motor cycle. The tunnel on the LWR then, was constructed using concrete with metal reinforcing around timber box shuttering. I considered various methods for producing tunnel portals but at this early point in my learning curve, decided to purchase the excellent mouldings produced by Tenmille Models. Suitably painted and moss grown these are still in position some ten years later.

Timber Construction

Of course for various reasons it may not be possible to construct a railway in the solid fashion just described. It may be for instance, that one's state of health precludes bending and heavy lifting and so timber construction to provide a waist high running line is then a viable option. Properly protected, timber will provide a pretty good running surface, but personal prejudice coupled with the damp weather conditions in my corner of the United Kingdom dictate my preference for posts to be of something other than wood. Plastic drainpipe would be my choice but one could use concrete posts or brick piers to support the line. Whatever your decision a concrete foundation for your supports will save a lot of grief. Please don't try to economise on posts and I would place them at between one and one and a half metre centres. Your timber track bed, by its very nature, will try to warp and it is important to brace it properly with timber set on edge underneath.

Obviously scenic options are limited by this alternative but please don't think that you are landed with a utilitarian construction that spoils the ambience of your garden. One can plant shrubs and climbing plants to hide the uprights but I have always been impressed with the attractive method employed by Messrs. Peco on their garden railway at Pecorama in Devon. The construction of the railway is hidden by small leaved fast growing box hedging. I know that it needs regular trimming but it can be trained to represent scale trees and foliage. Wider sections of baseboard can be provided for station areas and it is here that our modelling and creative instincts can be allowed full reign. Apart from the provision of appropriate buildings and structures we might consider cutting holes in the baseboard so that potted miniature conifers or even outdoor "bonsai" may be dropped into position.

Of course I haven't covered all the different ways of constructing a viable track bed. Old hands may well be indignant that I have ignored several tried and tested favourites and it may be that your ingenuity will find an original method that particularly suits your needs. In any case what we are left with at this stage is a level trackbed with all the civil engineering basics but running through a fairly battered garden. Before we turn to the pleasurable task of creating an attractive landscape around our brute civil engineering its time to investigate the various options for our permanent way.

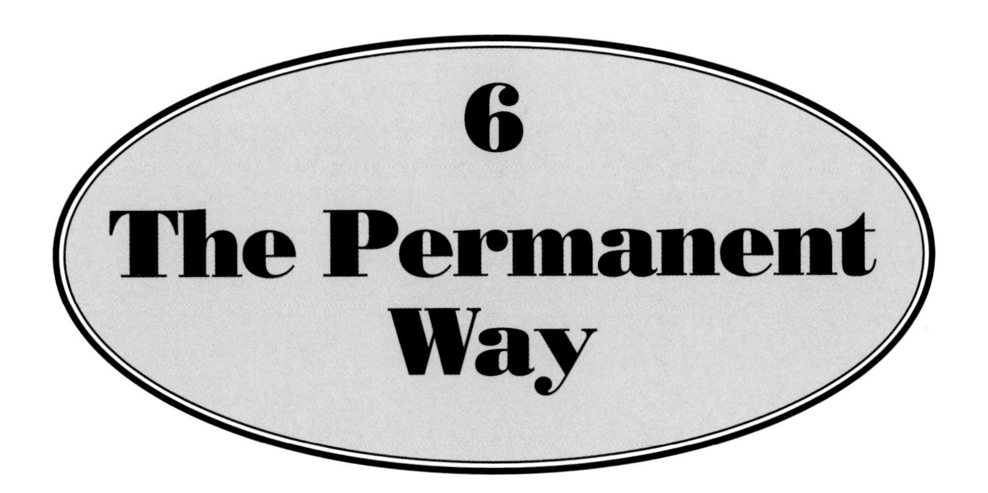

6
The Permanent Way

The scenic garden railway scales are actually quite well served by the trade in this matter and a wide and varied choice of track systems are currently available. There is no denying however that, depending on the size of your embryo garden railway, permanent way could be your most expensive purchase!

Elephant Proof

Perhaps the commonest type of track that you will encounter is a larger version of the standard plastic sleepered "flexi track" used in the table top scales. Really the only major difference between these and their indoor equivalents is that nowadays our large scale version is manufactured using inert plastic, unaffected by either the ravages of u.v. light or the extremes of the outdoor environment.

You will be aware also, that trackwork incorporating real wood sleepers is available in both flat bottomed and bull head varieties, for both 16mm and G Scale systems. Now that is an attractive thought isn't it - to run trains hauled by live steam locomotives over timber sleepered track smelling of creosote - but it has to be said that there are various constraints to be considered before finally deciding on the system that will suit your line.

Perhaps the most expensive trackage of all is the G Scale system marketed by Lehman GrossBahn. There cannot be a model railway enthusiast in the land that has not seen LGB's advertisement for their elephant proof track and well designed, good quality stuff it is too. It is also however, very expensive, and to my eyes the rail resembles scale girders rather than lightly laid narrow gauge rails, so perhaps it is more suited to more modern electrified or dieselised continential lines rather than a steam railway.

I would therefore suggest that unless you have a local infestation of

Maintained to Lynton & Barnstaple standards, this is the neat permanent way on Don Arthur's Tamarside line

Elephas indicus and a large pocket book it would be worth investigating other, more local, sources for decent trackwork. For instance Peco manufacture G Scale track with a plastic sleeper base, as do Tenmille Products and if you want the real wood sleepered G Scale stuff then contact Brandbright. All of these home grown products will cost considerably less and, in my opinion at least, look far more realistic than their Teutonic counterpart.

Floating Track

There are parameters other than cost that need to be considered when choosing trackwork. For instance timber sleepers, apart from requiring an annual treatment of wood preservative, will also need to be well drained. Many people like to "float" this sort of track in a properly ballasted right-of-way just like the prototype, conducting regular tamping and maintenance as part of their hobby. Nothing wrong with this of course and it is in line with the steam powered ethos of "the real thing in miniature" but it needs to be remembered that we cannot scale nature. Full size track has weight and mass to hold it in place and, while extra deep sleepers are available, its a good idea to pin track sections to timber battens to provide "grip" for the ballast. Minor problems with this type of track include possible rotting of sleepers if one is forgetful about yearly preservation and "popping out" of chairs, caused by expansion and contraction of the timber (a dab of UHU will solve this problem should it occur). If it has been decided to use spiked flat bottomed rail this last will not apply of course.

The commonest track in use today is the plastic sleepered variety, popular for its perceived ease of laying, "flexi" properties and suitability for flat non-permeable surfaces such as my concrete trackbed. A minor consideration is that the plastic sleeper web is susceptible to fire damage from fuel spillage if one is running spirit fired locomotives. Replacement of a damaged section of sleeper web is however a fairly simple matter.

Narrow Gauge Formation

If one is considering the purchase of this type of "flexi-track" then its probable that one's choice will be dictated largely by price. There are other differences of course and the rail itself can be nickel silver, brass or in some cases, aluminium. Now I live on the coast and have seen the effect that sea air can have on unplated aluminium window framing, so my options would be restricted, but both brass and nickel silver are easy to work and they weather quite nicely. The bottom line is that brass is cheaper!

Out in open country. This is the new extension on the Tamarside Railway, still showing the raw signs of newness

During this investigation of available permanent way systems do take a look at the range of different track items produced by the various manufacturers. Now there is no denying that the track supplied by Peco is well made and very smooth running, but in 16 mm scale they only produce a wye format turnout. This is termed a "typical narrow gauge formation" but really they don't consider it worthwhile to produce right and left hand points. If you are not happy making up your own handed turnouts from the parts offered by Peco then I suggest you look elsewhere. "Y" points are only really suitable for sidings or quarry type lines and if you incorporate them on your main running line then you will eventually and expensively have to change them.

It's worth remembering that your railway track is also, like rolling stock or buildings, part of this model of a narrow gauge railway. If one is used to modelling standard gauge steam railways indoors, then bullhead rail section with the appropriate chairs appears right. The fact is, that while the Ffestiniog railway had this type of track - and maintained to main line standards I might add, most narrow gauge railways muddled along with light flat bottomed rail pinned to indifferent sleeperage. The Longlands & Western has bullhead rail largely because I did not notice this obscure fact before purchase.

Family Effort

In many cases of course, compromises have to be made to reduce capital expenditure. As with most areas of human endeavour the trade-off is time, effort and a certain amount of ingenuity. Certainly costs can be reduced very significantly if one is prepared to do this and perhaps the easiest way is to purchase rail, sleepers and chairs separately, while manufacturing one's own pointwork.

If the decision is made to have timber sleepers then in truth it cannot be done any other way. The formation of track lengths for the LWR was a family effort with my young sons acquiring sore fingers from screwing chairs into thousands of pre-drilled holes! If one has plumped for plastic, then sleeper web can be purchased separately from the rail and kits for pointwork are also available.

Access to a band saw and pillar drill will make a considerable difference to one's outlay, but again with the time and effort trade-off. One can manufacture and drill one's own sleepers although, frankly, my heart would sink at the thought of actually doing it. I remember being very impressed with a gentleman from Yorkshire who actually manufactured his own 16mm track using home cut timber sleepers and with rail made from the metal banding used to secure bricks for transport to building sites. Including old engine oil to protect sleepers, the materials for this railway cost effectively nothing and while obviously not a scale model, it was the basis for a working narrow gauge railway and conserved precious funds for motive power.

The toy market can be a source of trackwork and perhaps the most obvious is that produced by Mamod for their Mamod Steam Railway. I know of at least one well known garden railway that uses this equipment, and with its sharp curves it is well suited for the very restricted site of the Budley Bumblebahn. It is not however, particularly cheap, and unless second hand equipment at a good price is available I would look elsewhere. Plastic trackage is, regretfully, unsuitable for steam locomotion but a small railway with battery powered "diesel" locomotion is a possibility.

Battleship Quality

Second hand equipment isn't always easy to come by and there can be traps for the unwary. Early Peco track for instance was quite badly affected by ultra violet and became brittle in sunlight. Other, even earlier types can be quite successful. Some of the track built for coarse scale O gauge is

Timber based trackbed on David Anning's railway currently under construction at Torquay. This type of construction will give long service if the timber is suitably treated. David's previous line was still in good condition on demolition due to a house move
(Courtesy James Slater)

battleship quality and quite suitable for narrow gauge purposes, although turnouts may well have to be altered to pass 16mm scale stock.

In the G Scale world some of the LGB fixed section items are quite handy for producing a smooth curve in a space restricted corner of the garden and, if determined on LGB products, the second hand market has to be the first place to look for affordable items. In general it's worth keeping an eye on the small ads in various magazines and occasionally, a tranche of unused track becomes available, sold on by someone who is waiting for retirement before starting their dream!!

Through the Wilderness

I construct and ballast my track a section at a time, for no better reason than it is somehow more satisfying at the end of the day to see the progression of the civilising railway through the wilderness. One's chosen method of tracklaying will depend to an extent on the type of civil engineering employed on your trackbed construction, so I am going to assume just for a moment that you have purchased "flexi-track" with a plastic sleeper web for laying on your solid trackbed. I shall further assume that your track bed is reasonably level. It would be easy to say that all one has to do now is to work around the line joining and screwing down the track but of course life is not like that! Garden scale track is larger and therefore harder to work and lay

than the equivalent N gauge on a flat and square indoor baseboard.

There is no right and wrong way to undertake this job and, for what its worth, I can give you mine. On a solid concrete foundation I lay my track held loosely in place by screwing into rawplugged pre-drilled holes. This may be through a sleeper or, if possible to one side, acting as a peg against the natural spring of the track. The number of these fixings is dependent solely on the curve of the track bed and I use the minimum that I can get away with. Of course each section on a curve is offered up prior to cutting the outside rail and using a hacksaw in situ is not recommended.

A Twist in Time

At this stage it's time to check, not so much for levels, but for the dreaded twist. A glance along the trackbed of the Welshpool and Llanfair line from the main road will tell you that a switchback route, in itself, is not a dangerous thing. Track twisted out of horizontal true on a tight curve is however, a recipe for regular derailment. The tools we will need for this job are a small short spirit level (I use a simple two inch long level supplied for levelling kitchen units) placed across the metals and a selection of grit, matchsticks, small pieces of slate or whatever, for sliding under the ends of sleepers.

The latest version of 'Lady Anne' pausing at Radford Dip. Note the cement ballasting. The signal box in the background is a product of the Welshpool Pottery

What we are doing here is not actually supporting the track - the ballast will do that - but positioning it with each rail exactly level with its consort. If you wish to be clever it is perfectly possible, with care, to actually set an amount of super elevation, but unless one intends running a narrow gauge Inter-Village 125 it is best to settle just for something that all the flanges of a narrow gauge vehicle will grip!

Damp Old Day

There are two forms of ballasting on the Longlands & Western and both involve the use of ready mixed sand and cement. You can buy and mix your own of course and save a few pennies but for the amount that one uses on even a very long line it is worth applying the controlled machine mix. My basic ballast and one that has been in use for ten years, is just plain sand cement mix tipped dry onto the track. This is brushed into shape to the level of the sleepers and one can leave a neat shoulder if required, before using a garden spray to soak it. This operation is best conducted on a British standard "damp old day" rather than during extremes of temperature. There are many variations and some people like to add a certain amount of peat to the mix to encourage the growth of moss or ground cover over the railway. I am a fan of bosky tracks myself and consider this mix, invented by David Rowlands, to be an excellent idea.

An LWR variant of this type of ballasting is to mix the sand and cement with horticultural grit. This give a friable well drained track bed, perhaps more suitable for timber sleeperage. It looks very good, is easy to remove or repair and happily carries the weight of the company's trains; however the occasional escaping piece of grit can get lodged in point blades.

You will soon get into the swing of laying and ballasting on plain track. On a long line a sort of rythym is developed and the permant way proceeds apace. At the end of the day one can stare out of the window with the satisfaction of a benevolent mill owner, happy with the efforts of one's industrious and efficient workforce!

Bosky tracks on the Longlands & Western. There is a concrete track bed under the greenery - honest!

Tallyllyn Adventure

There is no reason why wood sleepered track cannot be utilized in the same way as the manufactured plastic sleepered variety, by fixing it to a concrete or timber trackbed. Indeed, with certain provisos, this is what I have used on most of the Longlands & Western Railway and it seems to work pretty well. If I'm strictly honest however there are areas of the Longlands & Western right-of-way that have, other than the railheads, been covered with Sandwort and Corsican Mint these many years. The sleepers beneath have seen not a drop of preservative in that time and, like the early days of the Talyllyn adventure, I suspect the track is held to gauge by the vegetation!

In common with foundation and trackbed provision there are many other successful ways of laying track, far more than I can detail or even list herein. Further information is available via the back numbers of society and association magazines together with *GardenRail*.

7
Landscape and Terraforming

I venture to say that, horticulturally, there are two types of 16mm or G Scale garden railway. The first is a line running through what may be termed a normal garden, with beds of annuals, various flowering shrubs and of course - lawn! The other is a model railway running through living scale scenery. Your choice is almost certainly dictated by circumstances but there are certainly areas where compromise can come into play.

Now I have never been any sort of gardener! The propagatory skills required for nuturing a flower garden or vegetable plot remain a mystery to me and when, some years ago, I mentioned to my family that I was writing an article on gardening, reactions ranged from open laughter to the frankly incredulous! Despite this filial encouragement the article was written - with the result that some people found it useful and were kind enough so to tell me! I am still neither engineer nor gardener, but can make a good stab at fixing a recalcitrant steam locomotive and can also produce a reasonable approximation of scale scenery.

An Art Form?

In common with many people I enjoy a background of indoor model railways and over the years have devoured articles on all facets of model railway construction, including the practical and artistic skills of model scenery building. And of course, it is an art, with the modeller producing a four dimensional essay that is designed to purvey a sense of atmosphere and place to the viewer.

My friends we can do exactly the same in the open air. Few gardening skills are necessary and, like our indoor brethren, we can design our scenery as we wish. It may be of course, that you are a skilled horticulturist or at least an enthusiastic gardener. If this is the case then I could not presume to

Gnarled tree trunks and a footpath beside the track. Note how the small artifacts compliment the living green of the trees. Don't forget, it's not gardening - it's modelling!

advise on horticultural techniques but would respectfully ask you to look at your railway gardening activities from a slightly different perspective. For instance a riot of spring daffodils delights the eye and uplifts the senses - but these same flowers, nodding triffid like over our permanent way, effectively destroy the ambience of any garden railway. There is no necessity to eradicate or replace a mature garden, merely to scale one's plantings according to proximity to the permanent way.

Most people associate rockery with garden railways and generally speaking they are right to do so. Rock is the bone structure of our scenic endeavours and can be used, in conjunction with small stone, earth and horticultural grit to sculpt a believable landscape around our recently completed permanent way. The availability of stone or slate is obviously dependent on one's locality. In the granite fastness of the Far West stone is not a problem and most of mine was culled from the River Tamar at low tide. There are also several quarries within striking distance who will deliver literally tons of stone at a reasonable price - but do beware of garden centres who tend to charge a horrendous price for lumps of Cotswold.

As we construct this four

"A variety of textures......."

A Pearse 'Genesis' restarts to reverse up the bank. Fencing the line would improve this scene but I'm afraid nothing can be done about the full size fence in the background!

dimensional artwork it is worth moving our miscellaneous boulders around and, from different vantage points, viewing the results through half closed eyes. We have already considered practical particulars such as access to the permanent way and now need to contemplate more aesthetic considerations, such as observation points for just watching the passage of trains, or perhaps suitable positions for the taking of lineside photographs. I strongly believe that at this stage, we need to take the same sort of care as an artist when composing the basic elements of his painting.

As the bare bones of this embryo landscape take shape around the permanent way, it's time to consider clothing the 16mm countryside with suitable growing scenic elements. During construction of my Longlands & Western Railway, I determined to enlist the help of local green fingered neighbours but with little success. After some consultation it occurred to me that, while keen to help, they were looking at the modelling area as a twelve inches to the foot suburban garden, while my interests were in creating a scale living landscape as a backdrop for my passing steam trains. I therefore decided to investigate a local garden centre through the eyes of a railway modeller, looking for materials to construct scenery.

First Plantings

I picked a small area between the station platform and the Lyner bridge for my first plantings and set out for the unfamiliar territory of the gardening emporium. This method of proceeding turned out to be decidedly successful - although I have to say that most modelling budgets, including mine, could not handle the afforestation of the average garden line all at once.

These first horticultural purchases consisted of four miniature conifers, together with a selection of alpine ground cover plants. I conveyed these home in triumph and spent a pleasant afternoon posing the plantings to obtain the most satisfactory effect when viewed from the patio area. The trees and alpines were planted according to the instructions provided very helpfully on the attached labels, and several pieces of local granite were carefully positioned before sitting down to admire my diminutive diorama!

Texture, Shape and Colour

I had chosen my purchases for their varying shape and texture and this had worked quite well with the granite - but somehow, something didn't seem quite right. A vague memory of bonsai trees in bowls of pebbles flashed through my mind and I sprinkled some leftover wallspar on the bare earth between the trees and plants. A 16mm figure of a soldier kissing his girlfriend was placed beneath the largest tree and - it looked great! Serendipity had dictated that I learned lessons and made an important discovery that afternoon.

The first lesson was that stone, of whatever grade, looks good and is always in scale. My initial use of wallspar, while giving a finished look to the work, also supplied what is known in horticultural circles as inorganic mulch! This provides, if you like, a "blanket" for the roots in cold weather and also inhibits the growth of weeds while furnishing exactly the sort of environment in which alpine plants thrive. Of course we cannot scale nature and therefore miniature conifers are used to represent deciduous trees. Careful blending of texture shape and colour will add to the illusion but it is a good idea to "scale" a particular scene with a small artifact or figure. A fence perhaps, or a pathway with a small gate. Something brightly coloured such as a telephone or letter box is particularly effective, but easily constructed home built items like telegraph poles and small sheds help set the scene.

The railway runs through a landscape and is not necessarily the major feature

Alpines

Alpine plants are apparently a hobby in themselves and one should, I suppose, provide a list of suitable plants. I studied several articles on railway gardening and don't mind admitting that I was frightened by the lists of unpronounceable Latin names, and confused by the earnest advice regarding the care of all the various plantings. If you are a natural gardener then that's fine and you certainly won't need my advice - but if you are not then perhaps I can simplify things!

First of all we are looking for scale scenery not attractive plants! For instance one of my favourite effects is the dappling of light on the greenery beneath the miniature trees. Sure we can buy all sorts of alpines that will look quite effective on initial planting but will soon grow "out of scale". I would suggest choosing from the plants that look the smallest and most insignificant in their little pots. It was in this way that I discovered Corsican Sandwort (alright then *Arenaria Balearica*), the most commonly used ground cover on the Longlands & Western. Many of these insignificant little plants manage to have several names and another useful creeping thing is "Mind Your Own Business", alias "Babies Tears", real name *Soleirolia Soleirolii*. I didn't know the names of these little beauties when I first purchased them, and just looked for something small and insignificant.

Generally speaking garden centres or specialist retailers label their plants and trees. The label will tell you, very briefly, how to look after your purchase, how high it will grow or spread, and where to plant it. Many will also provide a photograph of the mature growth, particularly with alpines and this is useful. Very largely, this is all the information one requires. Some conifers for instance, are troubled by cold winds and the label will generally provide this information. If your railway is in a windy situation then take care that any susceptible tree is screened by other, hardier versions. Other plants are not particularly happy in full sunlight and again, the label will give this information - we don't have to be gardeners, we just have to read the simple instructions.

Bags of horticultural grit and peat mixed with the soil will provide a suitable eco-system for both alpines and conifers. Pile your rocks high and fill the pockets with grit, peat and earth. If, like myself, you relish bosky weed covered track, then chuck a bit of milk on the ballast when no one is looking and the sandwort will slowly creep over the permanent way.

Hacking and Slashing

Now I don't have any, but it is possible to purchase mature Bonsai trees suitable for the garden environment. These are I have to say, particularly expensive, but surely would look very effective as a backdrop to our small railway. I find ordinary miniatures expensive enough and afforestation of the Longlands & Western took over three years. Skills improved with practice and I took pleasure in planning my diminutive landscape, recreating dank tree hung cuttings and pleasant sun dappled groves. Ten years on the steam trains run through a heavily wooded countryside, the managed landscape providing areas to take photographs of visiting locomotives or just to enjoy the trains.

Of course many of you will know about miniature conifers and while probably perfectly willing to accept my description of tree hung cuttings, perhaps draw the line at sun dappled groves? Who am I trying to kid! Nevertheless it is perfectly possible to produce this effect and I would refer you to my suggestion that we are modellers and not gardeners. I hack my trees about with a pair of electrical snips as they grow and the simple trick is to cut from the ground up. The commonest mistake is to spare the knife, and I do think that it is actually difficult to cut too much away. Real trees have trunks that one can see. Real trees aren't a mass of dense vegetation that no light can get through. Real trees have plants growing beneath them, thriving in the semi sunlight.

In the 16mm copse by the LWR station starter signal, you will find heavy set gnarled tree trunks, moss covered rocks, a footpath through a wooden gate to the station road and a velvety carpet of "babies tears", sun dappled in the summer, softening the outline of the harsh local granite. It looks a nice spot, right by the railway line and must be I suppose, because the soldier is still there, together with his paramour, ten years on.

Heathers

I know this isn't a learned treatise about plantings, (I'm a modeller remember?) but I have to confess to a prejudice concerning heathers. The first resort of the rockery builder, heathers are I'm sure, purchased in their hundreds by enthusiastic garden railway people. I did the self same thing and very nice they look for the first season, but they are not suitable as trackside plants. I know that they have their attractions and for providing splashes of colour throughout the year a carefully planned portfolio of heathers will look very nice but please NOT beside the railway. They will eventually grow woody and disreputable and all of the many varieties I initially purchased for the line have been removed. Alpines on the other hand, have been largely self propagating and I have a working patch of "babies tears" together with "sandwort" and many a railway visitor has left with a spade full in a plastic bag!

Generally speaking alpine plants together with miniature conifers are the natural allies of the garden railfarer, and it was therefore with some pride that I referred my family to a newspaper article, which stated that this type of gardening was usually the province of the experienced horticulturist. I am rather glad that I didn't read that before "modelling" my scale scenery!

8
Buildings and Structures

The Pearse Leek & Manifold engine leans into the curve as it takes its train over the home-made bridge at Longlands

It may be small and strictly speaking go nowhere, but the Longlands & Western is for me a real railway, conducting its operations with live steam locomotives moving through growing scenery. It may today be damp, cold and inhospitable outdoors, but that doesn't preclude any enjoyment at all of our micro-world. A major attraction of the outdoor railway is that mood changes, with light and weather, are exactly the same in 16mm or G Scale as for 12" to the foot. A windless February morning, with watery winter sun struggling to disperse the rime of frost can be attractive in itself, but consider the plume of white steam rising high and straight from Longlands yard, or the chuff of a locomotive sounding sharp in the still cold air as it lifts a heavy mineral train up Trematon bank. Reflect also on the contrast between the rich, traditional colours and shiny brass fittings of this working steam locomotive, and the muted, frost edged textures of the miniature living landscape that it is passing through.

The point is that the railway and its environs are complete in themselves and it is therefore important that all buildings and railway structures are permanent and able to withstand the various weather conditions obtaining in your part of the world. A beautifully constructed and atmospheric station building is somehow spoilt for me if it has to be removed from its rightful place at the end of a running session. It has also to be said that one is unlikely to run that single train through our frosty February morning, if preparation also includes the setting up of all structures and their replacement indoors on completion. Not worth the fuss just for one train! That's what you would think, and it's a shame because, while no one would want to stay out in the cold all day, that single steam run in the sharp still air would be enjoyed and remembered.

The tea rooms at Hunters Tor. This model was constructed using fired "Stoneware" clay. The local pottery evening class were very interested in Graham Wilkins' reasons for undertaking classes. Note the prices on the menu board!

Building Works

Having started this chapter with my prejudices showing I should like to turn to what can be done to provide buildings for the new railway. Now I am certainly not going to tell you that all your structures should be hand built, or that commercial items are not suitable for the railway. There is an excellent manufacturing base, particularly in G Scale, and most of us will have seen the excellent but rather clinical Pola and Piko G Scale buildings. Easily put together, Pola could be termed the garden railway equivalent of "Superquick" and are just as recognisable. They can of course be modified to suit and experience tells me that this is an excellent way of personalising the railway. After all, what is a kit but a short course on construction! By all means, build from scratch if you feel like it - but if unsure of one's current skill level, or if you just plain like a particular supplier's products then go and purchase with a clear conscience! If, with a little more experience, one wishes to produce something entirely individual, then the experience gained in constructing the kit will be very much of use.

In both 16mm and G Scale there are various cottage industries providing appropriate buildings and lineside accessories and of course I can't mention them all, but I am particularly fond of the keenly priced range produced by the Welshpool Pottery. These are supplied ready coloured or prepared for painting and the imperfections of the moulding and firing process produce,

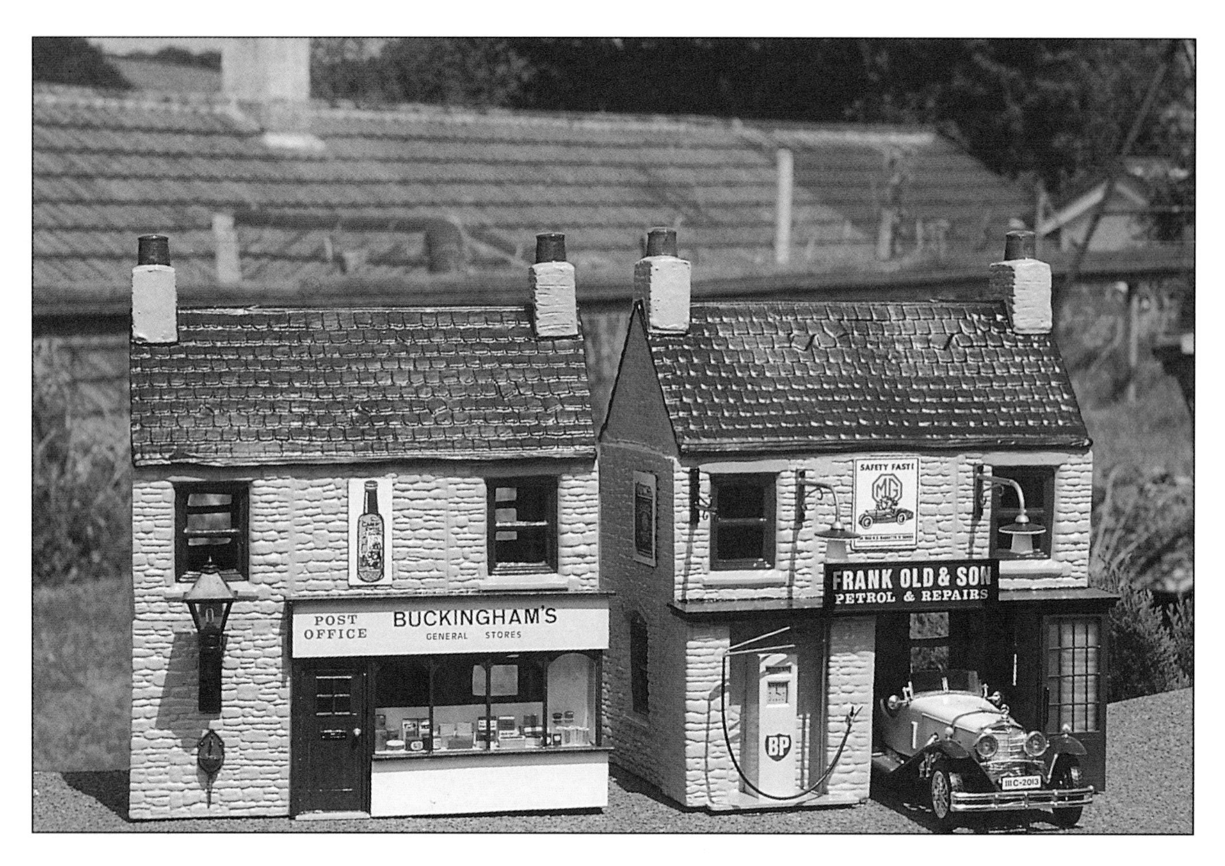

Two Welshpool Pottery cottages delightfully modified by Don Arthur

for me, a more realistic ambience than the soulless perfection of plastic. Local modeller Don Arthur has adapted these simple models to produce a series of superb and exclusive structures for his Tamarside Railway.

Garden Railway Specialists of Princes Risborough do some very nice Lynton and Barnstaple weatherproof buildings in British G Scale, together with a range of signals and sundry lineside items. If one wishes to produce something cheaper or more original, then R & J Feather of Todmorden provide a huge range of G Scale plastic veneer sheets including brick, stone and planking, together with station windows and doors. In 16mm perhaps the most popular kits are the range of timber lineside buildings produced by Brandbright Ltd. Most 16mm lines have at least one of these nicely designed kits, either modified or at least suitably painted in the company's colours.

Jigstones

One of the most interesting recent advances in garden scale real estate construction has been the development of the "Jigstones" System, available for both 16mm and G, which uses modular castings of quick drying cement to produce buildings and structures in various types of stone and brick, with window and door components cast in Isopon. Almost a hobby in itself, this versatile system can be utilised to produce very cheap and effective models whilst having the ability to provide colloquial architecture and an individual "house style" for one's railway structures. The Plymstock and Hooe Light Railway in Plymouth is justly famous for the large number of "Jigstones" buildings within its confines.

There are also individual builders who produce work to a very high standard. Modeller Stuart Currie constructs individually hand made buildings that could be fairly called works of art, employing a clay which fires to a Cotswold stone colour. These are fairly Rolls-Royce, and few people could afford to fill a garden with them, nevertheless using one as a centrepiece of a particular scenic section could well be an option.

Harmonious Design

Which brings me neatly to a reminder of what we are trying to do. In the garden it is easy to consider buildings and structures in isolation because by their very nature, they are separate from plants or trees. On the indoor railway this is just not the case. Buildings and greenery are constructed from the same artificial materials and are generally considered as an artistic whole. We should be doing the same in the garden with trees and buildings, plants and structures planned on our landscape as a harmonious entity. Try placing an artificial object such as a small shed, a telephone box or a 16mm figure amongst the trees or rocks and note how it "scales" the scene.

Many skills ported from the tabletop are useful of course. Consider the scenic break and the division of a modelling area into set-piece displays. Note how the eye is drawn naturally to particular parts of the layout by the virtuosity of the modeller. O/K I draw the line at constructing an outdoor fiddle yard, but what we are doing here is producing a work of art in several dimensions - and there is no shame in borrowing techniques from other, longer established scales.

Simple Structures

While currently you may have no intention of "scratchbuilding" any sort of structure it is almost a racing certainty that you will. One of the joys, for me at least, is that simple modelling somehow looks better than the most highly detailed commercial structure in the garden. Your first attempt may be something as simple as post and wire (or cat-gut) fencing. A simple thing in itself but, bearing in mind the legal requirement in this country for the permanent way to be fenced, you will be surprised at the realistic effect thus generated.

Narrow gauge lines are, almost by definition, light railways according to the Act, and therefore it is perfectly prototypical to construct simple

Sunshine and shadows dapple the Jigstone creations of Jacquie Mckie on the Plymstock & Hooe Light Railway as George's kit built 'Lady Anne' pauses for water

structures such as corrugated "iron" station buildings and timber built water tanks. Many of my early efforts on the railway company side of the fence were constructed using sheets of plastic corrugated sheet from the Brandbright catalogue, internally braced with timber strip and literally stuck together with UHU glue! Windows and doors were obtained from the same source and the buildings painted tar black. Now this cannot by any stretch of the imagination be called best practice but, sealed to a concrete base with external quality silicone, these simple structures are still in use some nine years later.

Of course I didn't get it right first time! I discovered that automotive sprays do not last all that long (I should have known this by the speed with which my motorcars deteriorate) and Sandtex was the best paint to use for this purpose. A worthwhile tip is that Sandtex may be obtained at DIY stores in "taster" pots at around 90p - no good for painting your garden wall but an ideal size for your diminutive railway buildings!

Another structure that you will almost certainly build from scratch is the bridge. It is possible to purchase these items, at a price of course, but generally one requires a custom structure for a particular site. The Longlands & Western girder bridge across the River Lyner (in truth my garden path) is constructed from aluminium angle purchased at B&Q then cut to shape with a baby hacksaw and bolted together utilising a table mat as a template. The whole, including paint, cost less than a fiver.

Prospecting for Gold

Generally speaking if one models in other scales then almost all purchases are made from a specialist model shop. Once the move is made to 16mm or G Scale, then all sorts of items can be pressed into service in the garden. A well known 16mm modeller got into the habit of carrying around a 16mm figure to "scale" items that might be of interest. Toy shops, gift shops and car boot sales are all grist to the mill and over the years I have developed a truffle hound mentality. The current craze for toy figures based on popular TV programmes has been a boon, and many a star wars or military figure shorn of weapons, has led a better life driving a 16mm steam locomotive! I have one of the old police boxes in Station Road at Longlands and I'm afraid I couldn't resist a "Doctor Who" figurine, complete with umbrella and this, together with the "snogging soldier" is a favourite with the ladies.

Of course it is not always possible to have structures permanently out of doors. It may be for instance, that part of your household consists of boisterous young children and it would be manifestly unfair to constrain their use of the garden.

Jigstones, Welshpool Potteries and home-made crossing gates at Trematon Halt. James the red engine (a Mamod conversion) pauses at the station

Do not despair however. The well known garden line at Hampton Loade on the Severn Valley Railway is built on land open to the public. Buildings are necessarily positioned before each running session and even signals are designed to be "planted" each time. A certain amount of structural strength is required for handling but this attractive layout attracts much interest on Sunday afternoons. Garden railways are a hobby for life and bear in mind that one can consider permanent structures when the children develop other interests away from the ancestral acres.

One could produce a complete book on this sub-hobby of producing a miniature landscape and here I can only scratch the surface but articles in *GardenRail* or *16mm Today* will provide a steady stream of inspiration in this department.

I look forward in the future to seeing *your* ideas in print.

9
Carriage and Wagon Works

It was ever thus! Motive power has always been the prime source of interest for modellers no matter what the scale or gauge - and rolling stock has tended to be an afterthought. In the model world, freight or passenger cars tend to be the excuse for running the engine rather than the reason! Some years ago, when my interest turned from trying to find some space in our small family home for an N gauge layout, to investigating the possibilities of radio controlled live steam in the garden, the photographs in *16mm Today* seemed to indicate that most people ran the same design of rolling stock behind their locomotives. Perhaps, in those days, doing it in the garden was different enough!

An overview of rolling stock in the garden scales, of necessity, needs to be divided into the two scales. While, in other areas of modelling, G and 16mm can be considered together, the divergence in approach of the two scales is particularly marked in this matter of a train to pull.

16mm Kits

In the early years of 16mm live steam modelling there was little choice - you built your own. Commercial support was minimal, although Archangel models produced a small selection of simple but rugged coaches and wagons to complement their range of live steamers, these had only a nodding acquaintance with the prototype. This was to be the way of it for some time in the early years. Merlin locomotives provided a choice of wooden kits designed by Donald Pearse. Based on Welshpool prototypes, these kits now much refined, are produced by Brandbright Ltd at their factory in Norfolk.

To assist with the commercial shortfall, the estimable Association of 16mm Narrow Gauge Modellers had a bit of a think and decided that cutting out accurate window and door apertures was the most boring and painstaking element of rolling stock construction. Accordingly a range of kits representing Vale of Rheidol and Glyn Valley prototypes were produced, consisting of sides and ends only, for the criminally low price of £1:50 each. Now out of production one was sad to see these go, but with the huge increase in trade support it was no longer necessary for the Association to act as a supplier. I do however, have a secret store of these kits in my garden shed, and a new rake of coaches is planned in the near future.

Building kits in this scale is a pleasurable business, even for those of us who have never attempted such a thing. The satisfying size and heft of a 16mm coach means that we do not need the skill, or eyesight, of a watchmaker to produce a good result. Certainly construction of some of the simpler wooden kits provides, as well as completed items of rolling stock, a short course in scratch building. Most of the materials are after all, available locally, and even simple compensated bogies are well within the range of the beginner. It should be remembered that this rolling stock is designed to run in the rough and tumble of the garden environment and solidity is prized more than a high level of delicate detail. The realism of your train is provided by the model emulating the real thing in the open air and, particularly on a video comparison, I have not seen an indoor model match the sight and sound of our real miniature outdoor world.

I know that many people in the smaller scales, while happy to construct buildings and scenery, tend to baulk at the construction of kit built rolling stock. Certainly my skills in this direction, particularly with N gauge models, did not stand up to the pitiless stare of the camera lens! The "handleability" of garden size stock on the other hand, is a real advantage to those of us with ten thumbs. Construction tends to be fairly pleasurable and the results easy on the eye. Do give it a try!

There is little doubt that, in common with trends in motive power, rolling stock items are becoming more faithful to the prototype and therefore correspondingly more expensive. There will however, always be a place for the simpler models in the garden, and a glance at the Branbright catalogue will show an array of rolling stock kits from simple plastic tipper wagons and wood framed trucks, to sophisticated and accurate models of Welshpool & Llanfair or Cambeltown & Machrihanish passanger coaches. Certainly if one wishes to build 16mm rolling stock from kits, then purchase of the Brandbright catalogue which has the largest range of these items in the world, is a must.

The exquisite Lynton and Barnstaple stock on Don Arthur's Tamarside Railway is constructed from modified Tenmill kits and provides an excellent example of what can be achieved with kit construction. These are highly detailed vehicles with full interior fit as per the original, and are complete with Edwardian light fittings. I have to say that Don will tend to avoid running these beauties when the weather is inclement, but as you can see from the photograph, even the £1.50 Vale of Rheidol coach is finished to the

A Vale of Rheidol bogie coach built from a £1:50 16mm Association kit by Don Arthur

same high standard. I'm afraid it puts my old and rather battered stock to shame!!

Scratch Building

The Budley Bumblebahn is probably one of the smallest lines in the country, and while Jim Slater's railway is justly famous for many reasons, we are here concerned with rolling stock. Jim has a collection of highly idiosyncratic home built stock based on prototypes from various countries and with a family resemblance that is instantly recognisable. Constructed using materials to hand, these are simply built vehicles which are long on ingenuity, short on

A rake of Brandbright kit-built coaches pausing at Radford Dip station. Note the awning produced by George Mckie using Jigstones moulds

Another product from the skilled hands of Don Arthur. This Lynton & Barnstaple coach was built from a Tenmille kit which Don improved with his own mouldings. I should like you to note the first class seating. All Don's passenger stock has period type lighting

cost and high on originality - this latter a feature highly prized in maverick garden railway circles!

With no sizeable manufacturing base, rolling stock for 16mm scale has been sourced traditionally via kit construction or scratch building. Ready to run rolling stock for 16mm scale is still something of a rarity, perhaps because the average kit is comparatively simple to assemble. For those modellers who do not have the time or inclination to do this, then Priory Carriages in Grange-over-Sands can provide a selection of ready to run rolling stock, including Isle of Man prototypes, which look excellent and Gratech Services of Gateshead also offer a range of well made R-T-R passenger and goods vehicles. Fortunately for those of us with more cash than time, there is also a fairly bouyant second hand market and the scrum around the sales stands at various exhibitions can get a bit hectic!

One of Jim Slater's modified Bachmann coaches. Rather a grand affair
(courtesy James Slater)

G Scale

There is, conversely a very large commercial foundation for G Scale, based of course on the electrically powered LGB system. LGB themselves provide a very large range of ready to run equipment and there is a huge amount available from third party companies. A glance through the American magazine Garden Railways will confirm that one is spoilt for choice, especially if, like me, you have a weakness for American prototypes.

On the other hand kit built items are very hard to find, particularly on this side of the Atlantic. In fact the only items in kit form readily available in this country are produced by Bachmann and these are basically the unassembled factory model. I should not like you to think however, that G scalers are bereft of imagination and modelling skills. "Kit bashing" is rife

More Bachmanns. This time the LWR directors' saloon and dining car hauled by *J B Earle*

and, if anything, scratch built items tend to be more detailed than their 16mm equivelent. The only problem with this area of endeavour is the comparatively high price of equipment with a continental prototype. One hesitates to take a craft knife to eighty sovs worth of LGB passenger car!

It was for this reason that I was particularly pleased to see the advent of the Bachmann American outline items at a very keen price and many a hacked Bachmann has formed the basis of a highly individual model. As you are aware I model in 16mm but I purchased two of these coaches to produce a pair of "Pullman" type cars for the use of VIP's. These consist of a directors' saloon with the seating mouldings removed and florid Victorian furniture added, together with a companion dining car. This item of whimsey would never have been considered but for the price.

Another advantage of the G Scale systems is the use of knuckle couplings for American stock or tri-ang type tension lock for Continental vehicles. Now I know the tension lock coupling is not aesthetically popular in any scale, but in terms of operating "hands off" it has the thick edge over the standard 16mm three link affair.

Traditionalists will be sharpening their knives after reading this, but certainly turning a twelve car consist on a wye with a live steam Pearse Colorado was pretty salutary. It certainly would not have been possible with a train of 16mm vehicles!

An interesting development by Garden Railway Specalists of Princes Risborough is the recent targeting of the much loved Lynton & Barnstaple Railway with model structures and a selection of G Scale rolling stock. This however produces a problem with scale and gauge. 45mm track represents a rather wider gauge than that employed by the L&B and certainly most British prototype live steam locomotives are built to 16mm scale. Having said that, I understand that GRS are co-operating with Pearse Locomotives to produce a live steam version of the L&B Lew .

One is allowed a personal opinion of course, and I prefer G Scale for American and Continental railways but use 16mm for our local lines. Largely this is because we have a very much smaller loading gauge than the rest of the world and certainly, with live steam, we need all the size we can get. People who model railways in the garden are however, an easy going bunch and of course you will and should, do what you want. No protofour/scalefour arguments here, because it is all about having fun - and in the last analysis, it's your railway.

There are several general points worth bearing in mind when considering the purchase or construction of rolling stock in either 16mm or G Scale. Large eight wheeled bogie stock, for instance would look seriously silly rounding curves of Mamod proportions. Take a peek at the photograph of *Jane* and her train of Mamod stock in chapter three. Despite the fact that the coaches are effectively tin toys, they do look "right" together. Remember too, that in these scales, goods stock can carry real loads. A rake

A pair of Bachmann coaches resting on a spur in the middle of Dartmoor! These have been detailed and weathered with consummate skill by Paul Fletcher

of four wheeled open wagons, when loaded with spar, will provide a very heavy train. This is certainly not a disadvantage and most steam locomotives seem to enjoy pulling a train with a degree of mass. Certainly, just as on the prototype, it can provide spectacular aural and visual effects.

One can also have fun with passenger stock and while one wouldn't wish to fill these with stone it is very easy to add weight beneath the chassis. I quite enjoyed adding luxurious touches to first class compartments and some of mine have padded velvet plush with varnished wood and mirrors. Of course one can't see it when the train is moving but I know it is there and this sort of internal detail can't get damaged!

One may be modelling a particular line or train and if this is the case then your parameters for livery are fairly limited. If however, like my Longlands & Western your railway is your own creation, then imagination can provide a livery that is right for your line. Now I have a problem with making more than two items the same so my passenger stock is a fairly mongrel collection. The livery is officially chocolate and cream (I am allowed to be parochial) but I soon became fed up with using the same colours and therefore hit on the artifice of purchasing stock second hand from other lines. If you visit the LWR then, do not be surprised to see coaches in the livery of the fictitious East Cornwall Narrow Gauge.

10
Last Train to Saltash

Ratty Matty, a modified Merlin Mayflower, posing at Longlands after repair and rebuild at the Gorton Locomotive Works (I couldn't resist that!)

The gas lamps at Longlands station glow softly in the gathering dusk and a yellow light spills from the booking office window, casting deep shadows beneath the trees. At the platform, the elderly chocolate and cream stock behind the oily Brunswick green and polished brass of the locomotive looks absolutely right in this location, less than a mile from Brunel's Royal Albert Bridge. As the last few passengers join the three

J B Earle chuffs slowly back to the shed at the end of a winter's operating session

coach evening train to Saltash Junction for connections to Plymouth and beyond, steam rises in a vertical plume from the safety valve of *Toni*, a venerable four coupled Merlin Mayflower and the company's original motive power. The driver is ensuring that there is enough steam for the difficult ascent of Trematon bank with this, the last train of the day.

It has been an enjoyable garden meeting, with some visitors travelling a considerable distance to attend. The afternoon has been busy with at least two engines in steam at any one time and the garden full with the animated buzz of steamy conversation. The session is drawing to a close and locomotives are being stowed away in their travel cases. Stock is replaced in boxes and goodbye noises are being made while tentative arrangements for meetings elsewhere are taking place.

As the final cups of tea are produced and young James Mckie demolishes the last piece of cake on the plate, the driver gives a short blast on the whistle. The regulator is opened and connecting rods begin slowly to move, as the last train of the day eases away from this bucolic outpost of narrow gauge steam in the West Country. Conversation stops as, with a steady and sharpening beat, *Toni* rumbles slowly across the Lyner bridge and attacks the steep curve of Trematon bank. Passing over the road crossing at Trematon and without pausing at Trematon Halt, the train disappears into the tunnel with a long wail of the whistle, leaving the steam of the exhaust hanging in the still evening air.

Its been a good day, a pleasurable day, and when all the visitors have gone and the loco is cooling from its last run, I remember the piles of magazines, the daydreams and the doubts of my initial faltering foray into this fascinating, sociable and wholly delightful hobby.

This is not a competitive activity. Even the events held at various exhibitions serve more to provide inspiration and ideas rather than assuage the competitive instinct. The shared pleasure of running living steam locomotives and exchanging modelling ideas at small garden meetings around the country, or the satisfaction of producing an attractive model, be it kit or scratch built, in the long winter evenings are all part of it.

While the hobby may be pursued at any level, even experienced railway modellers will learn new skills. For instance, I can now silver solder pipework for a steam locomotive, using a home made granite hearth and calor gas blowlamp. Once frightened of touching my first steam locomotive for fear of damaging this expensive purchase, I am now capable of rebuilding and refurbishing a worn out or damaged example with the insouciance of an engineer - although some of my methods would cause a real artificer to make the sign of the cross and mutter darkly.

The point is that one doesn't need specialist skills to produce an attractive garden railway that uses real steam power. If anything then 16mm or G Scale is, because of size and space considerations, perhaps an easier gauge to model in than 00 or N. We use real lighting and run in actual weather conditions and this will always produce a more realistic railway. Many people, including myself, do not consider their garden lines to be models in any case, merely the real thing on a smaller scale. Rivet counters are lost with the Longlands & Western because they cannot pick holes in the original - on the LWR things were always done that way.

In the United Kingdom we are lucky to have a plethora of steam locomotion. Preserved railways, summer operation of narrow gauge trains and steam specials on British Rail give pleasure to many. I am more fortunate than most because I have my own steam railway with locomotives hauling trains, as required, in my back garden. I have tried in this small book, to illustrate the opportunities available to those of us with more modest gardens - to convey the enjoyment and sense of satisfaction to be gained from building and running a small scale narrow gauge steam railway. What I cannot do is to provide the definitive tome for constructing and operating such a line. For of course there is no standard route to the perfect garden steam railway - if you are maverick enough to move into the great outdoors with narrow gauge live steam, then you will do it your way, picking the ideas you like from various sources, including regular publications such as *16mm Today*, *GardenRail* and *Steam in the Garden*. Our comparatively new branch of railway modelling is fast expanding, both in terms of numbers and the speed of technical development and it is still a great adventure - because you see, this is the real thing!

This then is the end of the line, the silver rails curve into the silent cutting, the lights are switched off and Longlands Station fades into the gathering darkness. Perhaps one day I shall see your steam locomotive running at a garden meeting and we will swap ideas and experiences over a beer or a cup of tea. Meanwhile I shall leave you with a simple quotation from long time garden railwayman John Tolhurst as, at the end of a busy and sociable garden meeting, he watched his Glyn Valley Tramway locomotive steaming busily into the setting summer sun with its long rake of four wheeled passenger coaches. He said, "I don't think I shall ever get fed up with this". So say I, John - So say I!

Steam through the trees. A rebuilt Merlin Hunslet pauses in the cutting